The John F. Kennedy Assassination

by Stuart A. Kallen

LUCENT BOOKS

A part of Gale, Cengage Learning

GALE
CENGAGE Learning™

Detroit • New York • San Francisco • New Haven, Conn • Waterville, Maine • London

LIBRARY OF CONGRESS CATALOGING-IN-PUBLICATION DATA

Kallen, Stuart A., 1955–
    The John F. Kennedy assassination/by Stuart A. Kallen.
        p. cm. — (Crime scene investigations)
    Includes bibliographical references and index.
    ISBN 978-1-4205-0110-0 (hardcover)
1. Kennedy, John F. (John Fitzgerald), 1917-1963—Assassination—Juvenile literature.
    I. Title.
    E842.9.K262 2009
    364.152'4092—dc22
                                                                        2008048914

Lucent Books
27500 Drake Rd
Farmington Hills MI 48331

ISBN-13: 978-1-4205-0110-0
ISBN-10: 1-4205-0110-0

Contents

Foreword

The popularity of crime scene and investigative crime shows on television has come as a surprise to many who work in the field. The main surprise is the concept that crime scene analysts are the true crime solvers, when in truth, it takes dozens of people, doing many different jobs, to solve a crime. Often, the crime scene analyst's contribution is a small one. One Minnesota forensic scientist says that the public "has gotten the wrong idea. Because I work in a lab similar to the ones on *CSI*, people seem to think I'm solving crimes left and right—just me and my microscope. They don't believe me when I tell them that it's just the investigators that are solving crimes, not me."

Crime scene analysts do have an important role to play, however. Science has rapidly added a whole new dimension to gathering and assessing evidence. Modern crime labs can match a hair of a murder suspect to one found on a murder victim, for example, or recover a latent fingerprint from a threatening letter, or use a powerful microscope to match tool marks made during the wiring of an explosive device to a tool in a suspect's possession.

Probably the most exciting of the forensic scientist's tools is DNA analysis. DNA can be found in just one drop of blood, a dribble of saliva on a toothbrush, or even the residue from a fingerprint. Some DNA analysis techniques enable scientists to tell with certainty, for example, whether a drop of blood on a suspect's shirt is that of a murder victim.

While these exciting techniques are now an essential part of many investigations, they cannot solve crimes alone. "DNA doesn't come with a name and address on it," says the Minnesota forensic scientist. "It's great if you have someone in custody to match the sample to, but otherwise, it doesn't help. That's the investigator's job. We can have all the great DNA evidence in the world, and without a suspect, it will just sit on a shelf. We've all seen cases with very little forensic evidence get solved by the resourcefulness of a detective."

While forensic specialists get the most media attention today, the work of detectives still forms the core of most criminal investigations. Their job, in many ways, has changed little over the years. Most cases are still solved through the persistence and determination of a criminal detective whose work may be anything but glamorous. Many cases require routine, even mind-numbing tasks. After the July 2005 bombings in London, for example, police officers sat in front of video players watching thousands of hours of closed-circuit television tape from security cameras throughout the city, and as a result were able to get the first images of the bombers.

The Lucent Books Crime Scene Investigations series explores the variety of ways crimes are solved. Titles cover particular crimes such as murder, specific cases such as the killing of three civil rights workers in Mississippi, or the role specialists such as medical examiners play in solving crimes. Each title in the series demonstrates the ways a crime may be solved, from the various applications of forensic science and technology to the reasoning of investigators. Sidebars examine both the limits and possibilities of the new technologies and present crime statistics, career information, and step-by-step explanations of scientific and legal processes.

The Crime Scene Investigations series strives to be both informative and realistic about how members of law enforcement—criminal investigators, forensic scientists, and others—solve crimes, for it is essential that student researchers understand that crime solving is rarely quick or easy. Many factors—from a detective's dogged pursuit of one tenuous lead to a suspect's careless mistakes to sheer luck to complex calculations computed in the lab—are all part of crime solving today.

A Long-Running Mystery

President John Fitzgerald Kennedy (JFK) was assassinated in Dallas, Texas, on November 22, 1963. But no one saw the person—or persons—who committed the crime. Only a few blurry photos and a handful of grainy amateur films—with no audio—provide a visual record of the tragedy.

Kennedy's suspected murderer, Lee Harvey Oswald, was himself shot to death two days later while being escorted by police to the county jail. Oswald's murderer was a Houston nightclub owner named Jack Ruby, who some claim had connections to the Mafia. Before his death, Oswald had proclaimed that he was a patsy, someone who was set up by the real killer to take the blame for the crime.

At the time of his death, President Kennedy had many bitter political enemies. These included influential members of the Federal Bureau of Investigation (FBI), the Central Intelligence Agency (CIA), and the U.S. military. In addition, the Kennedy administration was vigorously prosecuting several powerful Mafia bosses, including Carlos Marcello, a dangerous mob kingpin who "ran" New Orleans. In a secretly taped 1962 conversation, Marcello swore he would have the president assassinated.

After JFK was shot, it did not take long for investigators to begin examining the tangled web of relationships that connected Oswald, Ruby, the Mafia, the CIA, the FBI, and others. Thus began one of the longest-running mysteries in American history, still under discussion more than four decades after the actual event.

A Mishandled Investigation

Kennedy was killed in an era before the existence of digital cameras, camcorders, cell phones, and twenty-four-hour news

John F. Kennedy was the thirty-fifth president of the United States, and was in office for just one thousand days before he was killed in Dallas, Texas, on November 22, 1963.

coverage. In addition, crime scene investigators did not have the forensic science tools that they have today. For example, they did not have computers to match fingerprints, analyze evidence, or study DNA.

Even with the tools available in 1963, nearly every aspect of the Kennedy murder investigation was mishandled by the Dallas Police Department and federal agencies. Conspiracy theorists believe evidence was lost, manipulated, or even fabricated to frame Oswald or to cover up the existence of coconspirators. Others say there was simply no precedent for such an event and investigators were overwhelmed. The crime scene was large; it was filled with thousands of people; and there are dire national security consequences at stake when a president is murdered. In addition, investigators were concerned about the privacy of the Kennedy family, people who were treated like royalty by the press and public at the time.

Because of the way the investigation was handled, millions of Americans came to doubt the official government story that Oswald was a lone gunman. In the years that followed, professional and amateur investigators combed through the forensic evidence surrounding the assassination. They analyzed many aspects surrounding the weapon said to have killed the president, including the bullets, the fingerprints on the rifle, and so on. Audio and photographic forensic scientists studied a scratchy tape from a police radio and the amateur films showing the president being shot. Forensic pathologists studied the Kennedy autopsy along with materials that were preserved in the National Archives. Some even used forensic psychology to study Oswald to determine his motivations. The truth, however, has remained elusive. Despite the decades of study and more than a thousand books written about the event, there is still no agreement as to whether or not Oswald really killed JFK, if he acted alone, or whether he was involved in a conspiracy.

On popular *CSI* television programs today, investigators solve crimes quickly and conclusively. In reality, however, forensic evidence is often open to interpretation. In courtroom testimony, experts argue over the validity of fingerprints, firearm evidence, and autopsy findings. Even the accuracy of DNA evidence has been called into question in recent years. Little wonder then that the bungled Kennedy investigation, with its intense political overtones, is still the subject of argument among expert and amateur investigators. As each year passes hopes dim that the mystery of the president's murder will ever be solved. But if any more answers ever come to light about JFK's murder, they will come from forensic experts analyzing evidence from the crime.

CHAPTER 1

The Murder of a President

John Fitzgerald Kennedy (JFK), the thirty-fifth president of the United States, was dead within an hour of arriving in Dallas, Texas, on November 22, 1963. The volley of shots fired at JFK's motorcade lasted between 5.6 and 8 seconds. The murder of the president was a crime of such magnitude that it permanently changed American society. The investigation was handled in such an unprofessional, secretive, and baffling manner that many people lost faith in their leaders and trust in their government, feelings that exist to this day. Since the mid-1960s, poll after poll has found that less than half of all Americans believe the official story behind Kennedy's death.

If the crime scene investigation and forensic evidence were properly and professionally handled, it is likely that questions about the assassination would have been answered many decades ago. Instead, the event spawned a conspiracy industry filled with expert and amateur investigators who created countless books, Web sites, and films using every shred of forensic evidence to tell a different story. This led conspiracy researcher Jochen Hemmleb to write: "[The] Kennedy case proved to be a room with a hundred doors. The more I read about it, the longer I tried to understand its meaning, the more doors I seemed to open. . . . I found myself caught in a mess of opinions, theories, [and] criticism."[1]

The Open Limousine

One of the great mysteries of the twentieth century began at 11:35 A.M. on November 22, 1963, when Air Force One touched down at Love Field in Dallas on a warm and sunny day. The forty-six-year-old president and his wife, Jacqueline Kennedy, came to Dallas to strengthen political support

for Kennedy's second run for president in 1964. Texas was expected to play an important role in the next election. Kennedy's vice president, Lyndon Baines Johnson (LBJ), was a popular Texas native, but the state's electoral votes had gone to the president's opponent in 1960.

President Kennedy in the Dallas motorcade moments before he was assassinated.

Kennedy was scheduled to give a speech to twenty-five hundred local business and civic leaders at a luncheon at the Dallas Trade Mart convention center. He was joined in the blue presidential limousine, a 1961 Lincoln four-door convertible, by First Lady Jacqueline Kennedy, Texas governor John Connally, and the governor's wife Nellie. During the short drive to the Trade Mart, the president and the First Lady sat in the back seat while Connally and his wife sat on fold-down "jump seats" in front of the Kennedys. Secret Service agent William Greer was at the wheel.

Although the presidential limo had a clear, plastic "bubble top," the bubble top was not bulletproof, but it did provide some protection for the president. Despite safety concerns expressed by Secret Service agents, the president ordered the bubble top removed so he could ride through the streets of Dallas in an open limousine. Kennedy enjoyed riding through crowds waving and shaking hands.

Critics in Dallas

The president was extremely popular across most of the United States, but Dallas was not a friendly town to Kennedy. Many who lived there harshly criticized JFK for his support of racial integration, a ban on nuclear testing, and diplomatic negotiations with the Soviet Union and other communist governments. For this reason Dallas had been dubbed the "City of Hate" by the press because many of its leading citizens routinely denounced the president.

In fact, on the day Kennedy arrived, the *Dallas Morning News* ran a full-page ad placed by three businessmen that shrilly criticized the president and accused him of being "soft on Communists . . . and ultra-leftists in America."[2] Even before the motorcade began, handbills were circulated throughout the crowd that showed a profile and a front view of President Kennedy, similar to a police mug shot, with a caption that read "Wanted For Treason: This Man Is Wanted for Treasonous Activities Against the United States."[3]

Shots were fired after Kennedy's limousine passed the Texas School Book Depository, pictured, and reached Dealey Plaza.

All the President's Enemies

When John F. Kennedy arrived in Dallas on November 22, 1963, the Secret Service was extremely worried about the president's safety. Kennedy had made many enemies in his one thousand days in office.

Kennedy's enemies can be traced to events that took place months before his 1960 election. In January 1959 communist revolutionary Fidel Castro overthrew the Cuban government in a coup ousting a repressive dictator who was friendly to the United States. In the aftermath, Castro shut down hundreds of casinos, nightclubs, and houses of prostitution that had been making millions for the Mafia for decades.

In the United States, CIA officials made plans to oust Castro, fearing he would allow the Soviet Union to establish military bases on the island 90 miles (145km) from Florida. The CIA trained fourteen hundred Cuban exiles to invade Cuba in a southwest region known as the Bay of Pigs. They were to be aided by the U.S. Air Force, which would drop bombs on Cuban military targets. The paramilitary force was ready to attack Castro in April 1961 several months after Kennedy was inaugurated. The president, however, called off the American air strikes at the last minute and the anti-Castro forces were quickly defeated by the Cuban military. Having failed, the CIA went on to make plans with Mafia hit men to kill Castro. When Kennedy heard about these illegal schemes, he fired CIA director Allen Dulles and vowed to smash the CIA into a thousand pieces. Conspiracy researchers believe any number of people associated with anti-Castro Cubans, the Mafia, or the CIA could have participated in JFK's assassination.

Despite the negative political atmosphere, the streets were lined with adoring crowds as Kennedy's limousine headed through downtown Dallas. The presidential motorcade turned right from Main Street onto Houston Street, drove one block, then made a sharp left onto Elm Street. In order

to make this final 120-degree turn the presidential motorcade was forced to slow down to 11 miles per hour (18kph). This maneuver violated Secret Service regulations which stated that a motorcade should always maintain speeds of 20 miles per hour (32kph) or more to maintain the president's safety.

The limousine slowed further as it coasted down the inclined street in front of the seven-story Texas School Book Depository, a book distribution warehouse. The president and First Lady smiled and waved at the enthusiastic crowds. Mrs. Connally turned to the president and said, "Mr. President, you can't say that Dallas doesn't love you." Kennedy replied, "That's obvious."[4]

Once past the Book Depository, the motorcade approached a small grassy area called Dealey Plaza, named after George Bannerman Dealey, founding publisher of the *Dallas Morning News*. This small, 3-acre (1.2ha) park is bordered on the west by a railroad bridge known as the Triple Underpass because three streets converge to pass under it.

About three cars ahead of the presidential limousine, Secret Service agent Winston G. Lawson radioed ahead to the Trade Mart and said the motorcade would be arriving in five minutes. To the president's right, a small hill now known as the "grassy knoll," rose at the back of Dealey Plaza. At the top of the grassy knoll a picket fence extended from a passageway of columns called a colonnade. These slight barriers separated Dealey Plaza from a busy railroad yard and dirt parking lot used by the Sheriff's Department.

Gunfire Fills the Air

Twelve seconds after a large clock on a billboard atop the Book Depository changed to 12:30 P.M., the sound of gunfire filled the air. In his book *Conspiracy*, Anthony Summers describes the sequence of events that followed:

> According to a Secret Serviceman in the car, the President . . . lurched in his seat, both hands clawing toward his throat. Directly in front of the President, Governor Connally heard one shot and was then hit himself. He screamed. . . . Then came more gunfire. The President fell violently backwards and to his left, his head exploding in a halo of brain tissue, blood and bone. To Mrs. Connally it "was like buckshot falling all over us." As the car finally gathered speed, Mrs. Kennedy believed she cried, "I love you, Jack." From the front seat the Governor's wife heard her exclaim, "Jack . . . they've killed my husband," then "I have his brains in my hand." This last Mrs. Kennedy repeated time and time again.[5]

During the shooting, Governor Connally sustained wounds in his back, right chest, right wrist, and left thigh. As the bullets rained down, Agent Clint Hill, who had been running behind the car, jumped on the bumper of the limousine and crawled up on the trunk to block the president and Mrs. Kennedy from further shots.

The barrage of shots lasted several seconds. After the sound of gunfire stopped echoing through Dealey Plaza, Greer accelerated, driving to Parkland Memorial Hospital where doctors worked in vain to save the president's life. Their efforts failed and Kennedy was pronounced dead at 1:00 P.M. Although Connally was badly wounded, he survived.

Searching the Book Depository

Immediately after the limousine sped off, chaos reigned in Dealey Plaza. Dozens of people had dived to the ground during the shooting, and police and federal agents were running everywhere. Some witnesses thought the shots came from

The view from the sixth floor window of the Texas School Book Depository approximately one hour after the assassination.

behind the picket fence on Dealey Plaza; others pointed to the bridge over the Triple Underpass. Many, however, heard the shots come from the Book Depository. Dallas motorcycle patrolman Marion Baker had seen startled pigeons flying off the roof of the Book Depository as gunshots rang out. He pulled out his gun and ran into the building about 90 seconds after the shooting.

Baker and building supervisor Roy Truly ran up the stairs in the building to the second-floor lunchroom. There they encountered Lee Harvey Oswald, who had worked at the Book Depository for several months. Truly later said "Oswald didn't seem overly excited or afraid."[6] Because of Oswald's calm demeanor, Officer Baker dismissed him as a suspect and moved on in his search for the assassin. Several minutes later, Oswald casually walked out of the Book Depository and boarded a city bus.

Other officers were called to the scene and about twenty minutes after the shooting, several police officers were searching the sixth floor of the Book Depository. Captain J. Will Fritz, chief of the homicide and robbery bureau of the Dallas Police Department, arrived to take control of the investigation. Authorities found three spent bullet cartridges in the southwest corner of the sixth floor, an area now known as the "sniper's nest." The shell casings lay near a half-opened window that overlooked Elm Street and the motorcade route. Moments later, police searching the northeast corner of the sixth floor found a rifle with a telescopic sight stashed between two pallets piled with cartons of books.

Oswald Arrested

As police frantically searched the Book Depository for the gunman, Oswald's bus lurched slowly through the heavy traffic produced by the day's events. Eventually, Oswald got off the bus and hailed a cab to take him to the boarding house where he lived.

About thirty minutes after the assassination, Oswald entered his small rented room, changed his shirt, and grabbed a Smith and Wesson .38-caliber revolver from the bureau. Although there were no witnesses, police say Oswald left his house at 1:04 P.M. and walked about a mile. Like other aspects concerning Oswald's behavior on that day, there are several versions of what happened next.

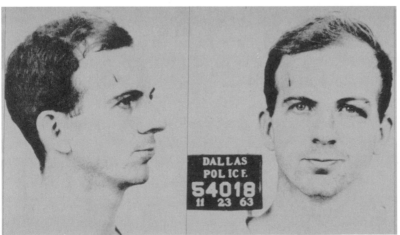

Lee Harvey Oswald was originally arrested for shooting Dallas police officer J.D. Tippit, who stopped him for questioning shortly after the assassination.

Steps in a Process: Interviewing a Suspect

How to Interview a Suspect

Investigators who interview criminal suspects must use psychology in tandem with quick, creative thinking. Investigators follow these procedures:

1 Engage the suspect in light conversation to judge their character. Topics may include their job, family relations, hobbies, taste in music, and so on.

2 Observe if the suspect acts suspicious, frightened, aggressive, overconfident, or is prone to bragging.

3 In the midst of light conversation, the investigator quickly switches to the criminal matter at hand. The suspect's first reaction often provides valuable information concerning his or her guilt or innocence.

4 Investigators let the suspect describe the case with no interruption. Often a fabricated story will be heavy on details since it was prepared in advance. Any inconsistencies, stuttering, or backtracking are noted.

5 As soon as the suspect finishes the story, he or she will be left alone for about twenty minutes to worry.

6 After returning, the investigator will ask about inconsistencies in the suspect's story.

7 Further questions will be asked about exact details, such the license number of a vehicle or the clothing worn by a victim. This allows the investigator to determine if the story has been rehearsed or overthought.

Steps in a Process:
Interviewing a Suspect (continued)

8 The investigator will observe the suspect for signs of lying which include rapidly blinking eyes, looking up at the ceiling, tilting of the head, crossing and uncrossing arms and hands, looking too relaxed, or sitting on the edge of the chair.

9 Investigators will remain quiet even when they notice a major inconsistency in the suspect's story.

Authorities say that around 1:10 P.M. Dallas police officer J.D. Tippit heard an announcement on his police radio. The suspect in the Kennedy assassination had been described as a thin, white male around 5 feet, 10 inches (1.8m) tall and weighing about 165 pounds. The officer saw Oswald walking down the street and believed he fit that description. Tippet stopped Oswald to question him. The officer exited his car and walked around the front of the vehicle to talk. Oswald allegedly pulled out his gun and shot Tippit three times in the stomach, killing him. There were several people in the vicinity who saw the killing from a distance but none were able to readily identify the shooter as Oswald.

Witnesses did see Oswald running into a nearby movie house, the Texas Theater, where he sneaked in without paying. When reports of Tippit's shooting were broadcast over the police radio, dozens of police officers converged on the movie house. Officer Nick McDonald found Oswald sitting in the nearly empty theater. When he approached, Oswald punched him in the face. During the short scuffle that ensued, Oswald tried to fire his gun at McDonald but it jammed. Oswald was finally overpowered by several police officers. As they led the suspect through the theater lobby, Oswald yelled at a news reporter "I want my lawyer. I know my rights. Typical police brutality. Why are you doing this to me?"[7] Oswald was transported to Dallas police headquarters. During the ride to the station, officers said the suspect was calm and collected, showing no emotion while asserting his innocence in the Tippit shooting.

A Highly Irregular Inquiry

Around 2 P.M., the patrol car with Oswald pulled into the basement of Dallas police headquarters. Dozens of reporters and photographers were gathered to see the suspect. An officer asked Oswald if he wanted a jacket over his head to hide his identity from the press. Oswald answered, "Why should I cover my face, I haven't done anything to be ashamed of."[8] When Oswald was taken upstairs to the third floor to be booked, the arresting officers only told detectives they captured the man who killed Officer Tippit. Upon searching the suspect's wallet, police found two forms of identification, one identifying the man as Lee Oswald, the other identifying him as Alek J. Hidell, an alias sometimes used by Oswald.

In the hour before Oswald's arrest, Captain Fritz had been notified by Book Depository building superintendent Roy Truly

Vice President Lyndon B. Johnson takes the oath of office of President of the United States aboard Air Force One, wife Lady Bird to his right and Jacqueline Kennedy to his left.

that Oswald was missing. Fritz believed Oswald, one of fifteen men that worked in the building, was the main suspect in the Kennedy assassination. When Fritz arrived at Dallas police headquarters around 2 P.M., he mentioned the name of the missing employee and discovered Oswald had already been arrested and was in the interrogation room. Meanwhile, at 2:38 P.M., little more than three hours after the Kennedys landed in Dallas, vice president Lyndon Johnson was sworn in as president of the United States. Standing next to him, a grief-stricken Jacqueline Kennedy looked on, her Chanel suit and white gloves caked with her husband's blood.

By 4 P.M. the third floor of police headquarters was in chaos. Officers were transferring Oswald to the building's basement. There, the suspect was placed in a police lineup where a woman who had witnessed Tippit's murder from several blocks away identified Oswald as the gunman. Camera flashbulbs popped and reporters frantically shouted questions at the suspect. Oswald, who had not yet been charged with Kennedy's murder, seemed surprised by the reception. When asked if he killed the president, he said that no one had charged him with that yet, and in fact, it was the first time he had heard of such a charge. When he realized what was happening, he told reporters he was being set up to take the blame for the Kennedy assassination, yelling "I'm just a patsy!"[9]

Oswald was led to Captain Fritz's office where he underwent intense questioning by city, state, and federal authorities. Dallas police captain Fritz took notes during his initial interviews but no known notes, tape recordings, or films were made during the subsequent twelve hours of FBI interrogation. The lack of an official transcript is a point of concern for conspiracy theorists. As New Orleans district attorney Jim Garrison writes in *On the Trail of the Assassins*,

> the Dallas Police Department . . . conducted a highly irregular inquiry. For example, after his arrest Lee Harvey Oswald was questioned while in the custody of Captain Will Fritz, head of the Dallas Police Homicide

Division. As a prosecutor, I knew that recording of such questioning is routine even in minor felony cases. Yet . . . the alleged murderer of the President of the United States had been questioned for a total of 12 hours without any taping or shorthand notes by a stenographer. Nor was any attorney present. The absence of any record of the interrogations of Oswald revealed a disregard for basic constitutional rights that was foreign to me. This could not be mere sloppiness, I realized. A police officer of 30 years' experience like Captain Fritz had to be aware that anything Oswald said under such circumstances would be inadmissible in any subsequent trial.[10]

A government investigation of the case later blamed the unorthodox nature of the interrogation on the general state of chaos in the station at the time. The interrogation room itself was packed with Secret Service agents, FBI agents, and Dallas police officers.

"He Wasn't Going to Say Anything"

The next day, Saturday, November 23, as a shocked nation mourned its fallen president, the FBI released dozens of facts concerning Oswald's unusual background. He did not finish high school. After serving in the Marines from 1957 to 1959, he defected to the Soviet Union, where he lived for several years. He then returned to the United States with a Russian wife, Marina. He spoke fluent Russian, a skill he learned in the Marines.

In the months before Kennedy's assassination, Oswald spent many hours handing out procommunist fliers on a street corner in New Orleans. In addition, a short time before the assassination, Oswald was said to have traveled to Mexico City, where he went to the Cuban Consulate and indicated an intense desire to move to Cuba.

These facts led investigating officers to conclude that Lee Harvey Oswald was a communist whose political beliefs had inspired the murder of the president of the United States. Some

A Fact-Finding Agency

During murder trials, defense lawyers use forensic evidence and testimony from investigators, experts, and eyewitnesses to cast doubt on the defendant's guilt. If the accused dies before being tried in court, then the case never goes to trial. Therefore, Lee Harvey Oswald was never tried in a court of law to determine whether or not he killed President Kennedy. This is addressed in the foreword of the Warren Commission:

> If Oswald had lived he could have had a trial by American standards of justice where he would have been able to exercise his full rights under the law. A judge and jury would have presumed him innocent until proven guilty beyond a reasonable doubt. He might have furnished information which could have affected the course of his trial. He could have participated in and guided his defense. There could have been an examination to determine whether he was sane under prevailing legal standards. All witnesses, including possibly the defendant, could have been subjected to searching examination under the adversary system of American trials. The Commission has functioned neither as a court presiding over [a criminal trial] nor as a prosecutor determined to prove a case, but as a fact-finding agency committed to [learning] the truth.

Report of the Warren Commission on the Assassination of President Kennedy. New York: McGraw-Hill, 1964, p. xiv.

suspected that Oswald might have even been working with spies from Cuba, the Soviet Union, or some type organization.

Oswald never had the chance to publicly explain his actions. Two days after Kennedy's murder, on November 24, authorities decided to move the suspect from the city jail to the

While being transported by Dallas detectives from the city jail, Lee Harvey Oswald is shot in the stomach by Jack Ruby, who leapt out of the surrounding crowd.

more secure county jail. At about 11:20 A.M., the handcuffed prisoner, flanked by several police detectives, was led through the prisoner transfer area in the basement of the Dallas Police Headquarters toward a waiting armored car.

The transfer area was in an underground parking garage that was crowded with reporters and onlookers. Despite heavy security, Jack Ruby, a nightclub owner who some say had Mafia connections, leapt out of the crowd and shot Oswald in the stomach with a .38-caliber revolver. Unlike Kennedy's assassination, this event was captured on live television. And since ABC, CBS, and NBC, the three major television networks at the time, had suspended regular programming to broadcast the breaking news, an estimated 175 million people—93 percent of all Americans—witnessed the shooting live that Sunday afternoon.

After being shot, Oswald was conscious for a few moments. Sensing this might be the last chance to talk to the suspect, Detective Billy Combest tried to communicate: "I got right down on the floor with him, just literally on my hands and knees. And I asked him if he would like to make any confession, any statement in connection with the assassination of the President. . . . Several times he responded to me by shaking his head [side to side] in a definitive manner. . . . He wasn't going to correspond with me, he wasn't going to say anything."[11]

Oswald was taken to Parkland Memorial Hospital where the same doctors who had tried to save President Kennedy now tried to save his accused assassin. Their efforts were futile and Oswald died at 1:07 P.M. He was buried in Dallas on November 25, the same day Kennedy was laid to rest in Arlington National Cemetery in Virginia.

We May Never Know

In the days following the assassination, Oswald's ties to Cuba and the Soviet Union were widely publicized in the press. This led many Americans to conclude that their president had been murdered by an enemy foreign power. If true, Kennedy's assassination was an act of war. During this era, known as the cold war, the Soviet Union and the United States had thousands of nuclear missiles aimed at one another ready to launch on a moment's notice. If JFK's murder ignited World War III, it would have likely led to the complete destruction of the human race.

In order to quell rumors and fears, President Johnson quickly contacted Soviet leaders, who assured him they did not plot to kill Kennedy. To satisfy the American public that there

A handcuffed Jack Ruby is led by police through Dallas city jail to his arraignment for murdering Lee Harvey Oswald.

Becoming a Secret Service Agent

Job Description:
U.S. Secret Service agents work for the Treasury Department. They investigate financial crimes, such as counterfeiting, bank fraud, computer and telecommunications fraud, and money laundering. They protect the president, the vice president, and their immediate families. Agents also protect former presidents, their spouses, their children, and visiting heads of foreign governments.

Education:
Aspiring Secret Service agents must possess a bachelor's degree from an accredited college or university, or have three years of work experience in the criminal investigation or law enforcement fields.

Qualifications:
Secret Service applicants must be U.S. citizens who are at least twenty-one years of age and younger than thirty-seven. They must have uncorrected vision no worse than 20/60 binocular; correctable to 20/20 in each eye. Applicants must pass the Treasury Enforcement Agent (TEA) written examination and submit to a complete background investigation which includes in-depth interviews, drug screening, a medical examination, and a polygraph examination.

Additional Information:
Any agent with foreign language skills will receive a one-time bonus equal to 25 percent of the basic annual pay.

Salary:
Between $26,000 and $50,000 with increases dependent on seniority, responsibility, and locality.

was no conspiracy, Johnson issued Executive Order No. 11130 on November 29, 1963. This order empanelled a blue-ribbon presidential commission to investigate Kennedy's assassination. It was headed by Supreme Court chief justice Earl Warren and was known as the Warren Commission. CIA director Allen Dulles, who had recently been fired by JFK, was one of the most controversial members of the Warren Commission because of his known dislike of the president. Other less-famous members of the Warren Commission included future president Gerald Ford, then a Michigan congressman, and future senator Arlen Specter. None of the commission members had previous investigative experience and they did not hire outside investigators. Instead they relied solely on the findings of the FBI and CIA to draw their conclusions.

Even with these respected government leaders in charge of the investigation, answers seemed elusive, prompting Warren to say: "We may never know the full story in our lifetime."[12] In addition, the commission was under pressure by President Johnson to produce a report quickly, before the upcoming presidential election in November 1964.

The Warren Commission operated entirely in secret and only visited Dallas briefly. It relied extensively on expert testimony regarding the evidence available at the time. On September 27, 1964, the commissioners released the *Report of the Warren Commission on the Assassination of President Kennedy*, commonly referred to as the Warren report. It consisted of a hefty twenty-six volumes of evidence and testimony plus a 726-page summary that concluded that Lee Harvey Oswald shot President Kennedy with a Mannlicher-Carcano rifle from a sixth-floor sniper's nest in the Texas School Book Depository. Oswald was himself murdered by Jack Ruby whose motive was to spare Jacqueline Kennedy the pain of having to return to Dallas to testify in Oswald's trial. The Warren report also states "The Commission found no evidence that either Lee Harvey Oswald or Jack Ruby was part of any conspiracy, domestic or foreign, to assassinate President Kennedy. . . . On the basis of the evidence before the Commission it concludes that Oswald acted alone."[13]

"Serious Reservations"

As soon as the Warren report was released, nearly every major newspaper and national magazine endorsed its conclusions. Most reported that the Warren Commission's investigation was thorough. Despite widespread media support, Robert Kennedy, the president's brother and the attorney general of the United States, stated that he had "serious reservations about the Warren Commission Report [and] . . . was open to the possibilities of a conspiracy."[14] In the following years, thousands of medical, scientific, legal, and law enforcement researchers came to agree with Robert Kennedy. They based this on inconsistencies they found in the report and on the panel's refusal to release documents and evidence for possible third-party review.

Sowing Distrust and Confusion

When the Warren report was published in September 1964, nearly every media outlet supported the conclusions that Oswald acted alone when he shot Kennedy. While some reporters and editorial writers doubted the findings and publicized alternative conclusions, they were labeled agitators, "conspiracy buffs," and even enemies of the United States. New York Times editor Harrison Salisbury officially dismissed the conspiracy theories in the introduction to the Warren report:

> Frequently these [alternate] theories . . . have the objective of undermining the United States. . . . Some have been aimed at sowing distrust and confusion at home. Others seek to convey to foreign countries the image of a violent America, helpless in the face of dangerous forces.

Report of the Warren Commission on the Assassination of President Kennedy. New York: McGraw-Hill, 1964, pp. xv–xvi.

The first published criticism of the Warren report hit bookstands in 1966. *Rush to Judgment*, written by attorney Mark Lane, refutes much of the evidence presented by the Warren Commission. Lane decided to write the book after his appeal to represent Oswald before the Warren Commission was rejected. The attorney believed Oswald was innocent and, although he was dead, he was entitled to legal representation before the Warren Commission. In rejecting Lane's request, Warren stated that the panel was set up only to determine why Oswald killed Kennedy, not whether or not he committed the crime.

Released two years after the Warren report, *Rush to Judgment* was the number-one best-selling book of 1966. People were still deeply interested in the assassination of the beloved president. Rush to Judgment has since sold over 1 million copies. In the following years, many more books were published that reevaluated the evidence and raised questions about the Warren Commission findings, deepening the mystery behind the president's murder.

Conflicting theories place the blame on suspects that include Mafia hit men; Secret Service, FBI, and CIA agents; and even President Johnson. The various conspiracy theories were fueled by the government's refusal to release documents and the forensic evidence used by the Warren Commission. Some 400,000 documents were finally released in 1998 at the urging of the Assassination Records Review Board. Still, key elements were blacked out and others remain locked away until the year 2017. The secrecy left the public wondering about the motives behind the murder of the martyred president. And some questions remain unanswered well into the twenty-first century.

By the Numbers

4

Number of U.S. presidents who have been assassinated.

CHAPTER 2

Medical Forensic Mysteries

In the aftermath of the Kennedy assassination, the Warren Commission, the FBI, and the mainstream media repeatedly stated that Lee Harvey Oswald was the lone gunman. But dozens of eyewitnesses, investigators, and government officials thought that there was more than one person shooting at JFK on November 22, 1963. By 1965, 70 percent of Americans told the Gallup Poll, an organization that conducts surveys of public opinions, that they believed Oswald had not acted alone.

If anyone helped Oswald, or set him up as a patsy, there was a conspiracy. By definition, a conspiracy is a plan between two or more people to commit an illegal act. One of the best ways to prove or disprove charges of an assassination conspiracy is to determine with some certainty how many bullets entered Kennedy's body and from which direction. If the president was shot from the front and the back, or from two different angles, then there had to be more than one shooter. The number of bullets and the direction they came from can be determined by doctors and medical examiners who specialize in forensic pathology, a branch of medicine that verifies the cause of death in criminal cases.

The Warren Commission confirmed Kennedy's cause of death using testimony from the emergency room doctors who tried to save the president's life and from the doctors who autopsied Kennedy's body. They looked at reports filed by these doctors and they found nothing to contradict their conclusion that Oswald shot Kennedy from the sixth floor of the Texas School Book Depository. Some people say the Warren Commission relied on flawed evidence and ignored discrepancies in testimony, so their conclusions cannot be trusted.

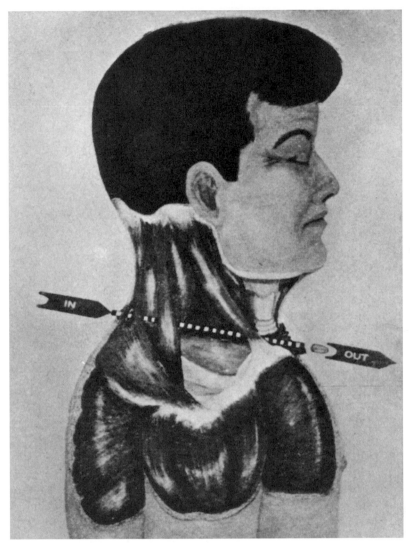

An artist's rendering of the proposed bullet path that killed President Kennedy used by the Warren Commission. This path supports the theory that Lee Harvey Oswald was the shooter, as the bullet enters from the back.

If Oswald had lived to stand trial or if others were implicated in the murder, then the forensic pathologists who examined Kennedy would have been called to testify in court. And attorneys would have used forensic evidence, such as the autopsy report, to convict or exonerate Oswald and any other suspects. Conspiracy theorists suggest that the medical evidence in the Kennedy case was mishandled so badly that the killer or killers might never have been convicted. Some say the evidence was manipulated to implicate an innocent man.

Emergency Room Observations

When President Kennedy was wheeled into Trauma Room One at Parkland Memorial Hospital at 12:37 P.M., he was already brain dead. A bullet had obliterated about 25 percent his skull and brain on the top, right side of his head. In medical terms, the president was missing the occipital parietal portion of the right hemisphere of the brain. Despite his condition, Kennedy continued to breathe as the twelve doctors and five nurses struggled to save his life.

Surgeon Charles A. Crenshaw was a resident at Parkland that day. (Residency is a period of specialized training when a graduate of medical school practices under the supervision of an experienced doctor.) In his three-year residency at Parkland, Crenshaw had treated hundreds of shooting victims. He noted that a bullet had entered the president's neck and pierced his windpipe.

In Crenshaw's recollection, the wound on the front of Kennedy's throat appeared smaller than the wound at the back. He believed, and later reported, that the throat wound was made by a bullet that entered from the front. In addition, the doctor believed the bullet that struck the president's head also came from in front of the limousine, not from the Texas School Book Depository, which was located behind Kennedy at the time of the shooting. As Crenshaw explains in *Trauma Room One*,

> I walked to the President's head to get a closer look. The right occipital parietal portion of his brain appeared to be gone. It looked like . . . an empty cavity. . . . From the damage I saw, there was no doubt in my mind that the bullet had entered the head through the front, and as it passed through his cranium, the missile obliterated . . . all of the parietal and occipital lobes. . . . The wound resembled a deep furrow in a freshly plowed field. Several years later when I viewed slow-motion films of the bullet striking the President, the physics of the head being thrown back provided final and complete confirmation of a frontal entry by the bullet.[15]

Rev. Oscar Huber of Holy Trinity Catholic Church in Dallas administered last rites to a dying Kennedy in Trauma Room One at Parkland Memorial Hospital.

Health Care Was Very Different

Before the assassination of John F. Kennedy, the medical records of presidents were largely kept secret. When the mortally wounded president was brought to Parkland Memorial Hospital on November 22, 1963, doctors did not even know his blood type. But things have changed dramatically as a result of the assassination. Today, whenever a president travels, a hospital in the destination city is required to maintain an operating room with a fully equipped trauma and surgical staff that has been fully informed of the president's medical history. In his book Trauma Room One, *Dr. Charles A. Crenshaw discusses what health care was like in 1963 when he treated Kennedy after the shooting:*

When John F. Kennedy came to Dallas [in 1963], health care was very different from what it is today [2001], especially in the treatment of trauma-related injuries. Ambulances were hearses equipped with a single tank of oxygen, and there were no emergency technicians. Blood from African Americans was not allowed to be transfused into whites, and vice versa. Other hospitals in Dallas didn't want to treat trauma cases because they were a money-losing proposition. A hospital's entire annual budget for such care could be, and many times was, spent on a few patients. And there were no such programs as Medicare or Medicaid. Mostly, we were treating the poor and underprivileged. Given the choice, a person of any means would never have chosen to go to Parkland because of its reputation—that is, unless he was in need of trauma care, in which case Parkland Hospital substantially improved his chances for survival. Otherwise, the selection would have been a private hospital.

Charles A. Crenshaw, *Trauma Room One*. New York: Paraview, 2001, p. 25.

Several other doctors present, including Ronald Jones and Robert McClellan, agreed with Crenshaw that the hole in the back of Kennedy's skull, about the size of an egg, was an exit wound.

After studying the wound, the doctors in the emergency room concluded that there was no way to save the president. Even if he lived, it would have been in a vegetative state. After several more minutes of frantic effort to save Kennedy, the doctors gave up. One of the physicians turned to Jacqueline Kennedy, who had recently entered the room. He said "Your husband has sustained a fatal wound."[16] It was 12:52 P.M. Someone covered the president's body with a sheet while a Catholic priest administered last rites.

Around 1 P.M. Kennedy was officially pronounced dead. The president's press secretary walked out of the hospital to speak to dozens of reporters, telling them Kennedy died from a wound to the brain, a bullet through the head. At 1:40 P.M. the world learned of the president's passing when CBS anchor Walter Cronkite interrupted the soap opera *As the World Turns* to announce the news on national television.

Inside the hospital, two employees of O'Neal Funeral Home wheeled an expensive, top-of-the-line brass casket into Trauma Room One. Kennedy's body had been cleaned and wrapped in two white sheets. Two nurses covered the satin interior of the casket with plastic sheets to protect it from being soiled with blood. Crenshaw was the only doctor left in the room and before he ordered the body removed, he reports that he took a last long look at the head wound before the casket was sealed and wheeled from the room on a gurney.

Later, when Crenshaw wrote about the events that day in his book *Trauma Room One*, he noted his observations concerning the wounds sustained by the president. Although Doctors Jones and McClellan testified before the Warren Commission, their observations about the exit wound at the back of Kennedy's skull were either ignored or overruled by other evidence. The Warren report states Kennedy was shot from behind by Oswald from the sixth floor of the Book Depository.

In the decades since the assassination, many medical experts have viewed the forensic evidence of Kennedy's wounds, such as photographs, drawings, and autopsy reports that were completed in the hours and days after the assassination. These investigations have come to many different conclusions regarding the direction of the bullets. Some support the findings of the Warren report and experts explain how the head wound might appear as it did if the bullet came from behind. Others believe the conclusions of the Warren Commission are incorrect. They say the head wound is evidence that Kennedy was shot from the front.

A Question of Jurisdiction

At the time of Kennedy's death, there was no federal law that made assassinating a president illegal. Whoever had killed the president was guilty of murder under Texas state law. In Texas, an unlawful death requires a justice of the peace to conduct an inquest, or a postmortem. In Dallas County, the justice of the peace was Theron Ward, who rushed to Parkland Memorial Hospital about three minutes after doctors ceased their efforts to save the president. Ward and other Texas officials attempted to take control of the investigation.

Texas law also mandates that before the body of any homicide victim can be transported, a thorough autopsy must be performed by a county medical examiner to determine the cause and circumstance of death. The Dallas County medical examiner was Dr. Earl F. Rose. But before he could perform the forensic pathology procedures required by law, a grotesque scene ensued in Trauma Room One.

Rose had already issued instructions to prepare Kennedy for a craniotomy, the surgical removal of part of his skull for examination. This was part of his legal duty, which also included gathering evidence during the examination of the president's clothes and, later, the scene of the crime. These investigations would help Rose establish how many bullets were fired and from which direction. However, by this time the emergency room and hallways were filled with dozens of military officers,

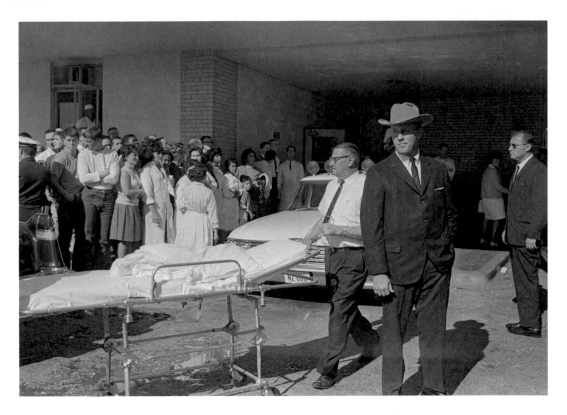

officials of the Kennedy administration, and Secret Service and FBI agents called "men in suits"[17] by the medical staff.

The men in suits tried to take control of the gurney with the casket. One of the doctors politely explained that pursuant to Texas law, Rose was required to conduct an autopsy. The Secret Service agents demanded that they be allowed to take custody of the president. Meanwhile, Dallas district attorney Henry Wade was instructing Rose by phone to search the body for bullets and preserve them as evidence.

The Secret Service agents were in no mood to deal with local authorities and attempted to forcefully push the gurney out of Trauma Room One. This caused Rose to scream, "We can't release anything! A violent death requires a postmortem! There's a law here! We're going to enforce it."[18]

As the First Lady stood beside her husband's casket, about forty men gathered around the gurney, yelling and swearing. Justice of the Peace Ward soon arrived on the scene and

Both the scene inside and outside of Parkland Memorial Hospital was chaotic after President Kennedy's arrival. Federal officials and medical staff were in great disagreement as to whether or not Kennedy's body should remain in Dallas for a proper autopsy, which Texas law required.

informed the crowd that it was his duty to order an autopsy. He added that it would not take more than three hours. One of the agents told Ward that it would not be right to put the First Lady and the president's staff through three more hours of anguish in Texas. After a brief tug-of-war over the casket, the Secret Service took control of the president's remains. Forensic coroner Charles G. Wilber discusses the implications of this move in *Medicolegal Investigation of the President John F. Kennedy Murder*. He writes:

> When the president was finally pronounced legally dead, there should have been a complete external examination of the entire body to catalog *all* the wounds visible and to describe them anatomically. [Instead Kennedy was] completely disrobed and wrapped in sheets for transportation in a casket. . . . There is every reason to contend that had the Secret Service and other federal agents not flouted Texas law . . . a proper . . . examination would have been made and in all probability the deluge of unbelief would have been prevented.[19]

The hearse carrying President Kennedy's body arrives at Love Field in Dallas as Secret Service agents prepare to load the casket on to Air Force One.

The Best Evidence

Kennedy's casket was loaded into a hearse and driven to Love Field by Secret Service agents. However, agents had neglected to order a forklift to load the large, brass casket onto the plane. Unwilling to wait even a few minutes longer for a hydraulic lift to be located, agents decided to carry the heavy load up the steep stairs of the airplane. However, the casket was wider than the steps, and it took considerable clumsy effort to get the casket onto the airplane. Once again agents ignored proper procedure as they roughly moved the body of a pre-autopsy murder victim. Their actions may have altered important medical evidence.

After landing in Washington, D.C., Kennedy's body was taken by helicopter to Medical Naval Center at Bethesda, Maryland. Despite the rough handling, Kennedy's body was

A Cover-up of Medical Evidence

Questions about Kennedy's brain autopsy came to light in 1998 when the Assassinations Records Review Board released hundreds of thousands of records from the National Archives relating to Kennedy's murder. During the partial brain autopsy, pictures were taken by a navy photographer. However, the brain photographs in the National Archives appear not to be of Kennedy's brain because they show much less damage than doctors observed in Dallas. This led Douglas Horne, chief analyst for military records, to conclude, "I am 90 to 95 percent certain that the photographs in the Archives are not of President Kennedy's brain. If they aren't, that can mean only one thing—that there has been a coverup of the medical evidence."

Quoted in George Lardner Jr., "Archive Photos Not of JFK's Brain, Concludes Aide to Review Board," *Washington Post*, November 10, 1998, www.washingtonpost.com/wp-srv/national/longterm/jfk/jfk1110.htm.

Steps in a Process: Conducting an Autopsy

An autopsy is a medical examination of a dead body conducted to determine the cause and circumstances of death. Autopsies are conducted in this manner:

1 The body is placed on a stainless steel autopsy table.

2 A pathologist conducts an external examination, measuring and weighing the body and listing all physical characteristics.

3 A deep Y incision is made in the body. The arms of the Y extend from each shoulder to the bottom of the breastbone. The tail of the Y goes from the sternum to the pubic bone. Then the skin is peeled back.

4 The ribs are then sawed off and the chest wall is cut away to expose the organs underneath. Organs are removed by cutting off their connections to the body.

5 The brain is removed. The brain is then either dissected or placed in a formaldehyde solution to preserve it for future analysis.

6 In some homicide cases or when there is a complex disease of the brain, a detailed study and dissection of the brain may be conducted.

7 All removed organs are weighed, cut up in sections, and studied individually.

8 Microscopic samples of most organs are preserved for further analysis.

9 All major blood vessels are cut open and examined.

Steps in a Process:
Conducting an Autopsy (continued)

10 The organs are placed back in the body and the head and body are sewn up.

11 The Y incision is sewn up.

still what conspiracy researcher David Lifton calls the "best evidence"[20] available to solve the crime. However, authorities did not bring in the best forensic pathologists in the nation to perform what was widely referred to as the autopsy of the century. Instead, the surgeon general of the navy ordered career military doctors James J. Humes and J. Thornton Boswell to perform the postmortem.

Humes and Boswell, administrators at the Naval Medical School, had, between them, only examined a single case of a gunshot wound before the Kennedy autopsy. As author Gerald Posner writes, "hospital pathologists such as Humes and Boswell are not trained in the forensic aspects of autopsies or the search for clues in unnatural deaths, nor do they normally preserve evidence for subsequent medical or legal proceedings."[21]

However, the doctors did call in Dr. Pierre A. Finck to aid them. Finck was chief of the Wound Ballistics Pathology Branch of the Armed Forces Institute of Pathology (AFIP), the consultation facility for the military which employed two thousand top experts in the field of pathology. This qualified Finck as an experienced investigator in cases of a medical-legal nature, involving trauma, violent death, a bullet wound, or an accident.

An Improper Autopsy

As the doctors prepared for the autopsy, the room filled with more than twenty nonmedical personnel, including admirals, generals, and agents of the FBI, CIA, and Secret Service. Because so many witnesses could distract doctors during delicate procedures, Wilber writes their presence was "quite contrary to medical directives and good autopsy practice."[22]

According to reports, these men were anything but silent witnesses. Several of those in attendance, were described by a witness, medical technician Paul O'Connor, as sinister-looking men in civilian clothes, took control of the situation. While conducting strident whispered conferences with one another about which directions the bullets came from, they ordered the compliant doctors to perform various operations and prevented them from conducting standard autopsy procedures. For example, one doctor testified that when he moved to dissect the wound in the back-throat region, he was ordered to stop. Without such a dissection, it is impossible to know for certain whether Kennedy was shot from the front or the back.

Such procedures violated the *Autopsy Manual* issued by the Armed Forces Institute of Pathology and used for all military postmortems. The procedures were also contrary to those followed by civilian forensic pathologists. As coroner and Warren Commission critic Cyril Wecht later stated,

> Kennedy's autopsy was "extremely superficial and sloppy, inept, incomplete, incompetent in many respects, not only on the part of the pathologists who did this horribly inadequate medical-legal autopsy but on the part of many other people. This is the kind of examination that would not be tolerated in a routine murder case by a good crew of homicide detectives in most major cities of America on anybody just a plain ordinary citizen, let alone a President."[23]

Liable to Court Martial

No one has been able to answer why the autopsy of a murdered president was conducted in such an unusual manner. Some offer a simple explanation. The entire event was out of the ordinary for all involved, and there was no legal protocol in place for handling the assassination of the president. Conspiracy theorists have formulated dozens of other explanations over the years.

Some believe the high-ranking government officials in the room were hoping to achieve their own goals from the

Forged Photos?

The photos of President Kennedy's autopsy were withheld from public viewing from 1963 until 1979 when they were released by the House Select Committee on Assassinations. However, the wounds in the photos do not agree with the descriptions given to the Warren Commission by autopsy doctors. This has led some to believe that there might two sets of autopsy photos and one set is a forgery. This belief is based on facts of forensic science.

When a bullet enters a body, it makes a smaller hole upon entry and leaves a large exit wound as it continues on its trajectory. Doctors in Dallas stated that Kennedy had a small entrance wound on the side of his skull and a gaping exit wound in the back of his head suggesting his fatal head shot came from in front. However, the autopsy photos revealed only a small, neat entrance wound at the back of the president's head. These images are not anything like the actual wound according to assassination researcher Gary Aguilar, who writes

FBI agents who saw the autopsy images of JFK's skull wound testified under oath . . . that JFK's fatal skull wound looked nothing at all like the photographs that showed the backside of JFK's skull and scalp intact. . . . Either 40+ witnesses . . . were wrong about JFK's rearward skull injury, or JFK's autopsy photographs were falsified in some manner to mask the rearward skull damage that these credible witnesses described.

Quoted in James H. Fetzer, ed., *Murder in Dealey Plaza*. Chicago: Catfeet, 2000, p. 189.

postmortem. For example, the CIA might have wanted the autopsy to show Kennedy was shot by several assassins who could be traced to Cuba, which would allow them to take violent actions against Cuban dictator Fidel Castro. The FBI and Secret Service, embarrassed by their failure to protect the president, wanted to promote the crazed loner theory, rather than a conspiracy which could have been prevented.

Some conspiracy theorists believe that CIA and military officials were complicit in the assassination. Wilber subscribes to such theories. He writes

> [it] is clear that those in charge were not going to permit the "whole truth" to come out. In this peculiar situation one must include the highest ranks of the Department of Defense, notably the Navy, the Secret Service, the FBI, and mysterious generals in and out of uniform … who seemed to have been giving orders that night.[24]

While the intentions of those in the autopsy room are unknown, it is a matter of record that all military personnel in attendance were sworn to silence under threat of arrest and ordered to sign an official document that read: "You are reminded that you are under verbal orders … to discuss with no one events concerning your official duties [at the autopsy]. . . . You are warned that infraction of these orders makes you liable to Court Martial proceedings."[25]

Respect for the Family

Conspiracy theorists have made much of the president's unusual postmortem and in 1976 and 1977, a congressional investigation into the shooting, known as the House Select Committee on Assassinations (HSCA) addressed this issue. After interviewing most of the men present, the HSCA determined that Robert Kennedy, Jacqueline Kennedy, and other members of the family were in attendance at Bethesda that evening and refused to leave the premises until the president's body was ready to be moved. This was barely eight hours after the president had been shot, and to expedite matters the Kennedys had only given permission for a partial autopsy because they wanted it over as soon as possible.

Therefore, during the procedure, Admiral George C. Burkley, White House physician to the president, was acting as an intermediary between the family, the doctors, and others gathered in the room. According to the 1979 HSCA report:

> [Dr. Humes] believed there was no question that Dr. Burkley was conveying the wishes of the Kennedy family regarding a full-versus-partial autopsy. [In addition] Special Agent [James W.] Sibert told the HSCA that he, too, had the impression the Kennedy family was somehow transmitting step-by-step clearances to the pathologists.[26]

Despite the conditions placed on the doctors, both Boswell and Humes claimed that they performed a thorough autopsy in the areas of the gunshot wounds. (A full autopsy would have involved a complete surgical examination of the president's organs and body cavity.) By 11 P.M. doctors had reached the conclusion that one bullet entered the rear of Kennedy's skull and exited the front. Another bullet had entered the president's back at the base of the neck and exited his throat. This wound was widened at Parkland Memorial Hospital by doctors who inserted a tube into it to help Kennedy breathe during the last moments of his life.

Because of the rushed and incomplete nature of the postmortem, several major mistakes were made. The areas where the bullets entered or left Kennedy's body were not dissected to determine the exact directions that the bullets traveled. And the angles of the bullet tracks were not measured to determine their course through the body. For example, Humes simply probed Kennedy's back wound with his finger, which not only changed the shape of the wound but, as most experts would agree, is also an insufficient examination to determine the exact nature of its cause.

X-Ray Mysteries

Further problems were created because of the way X-rays and photographs of the autopsy were handled. The official photographs would have provided an unimpeachable record of the autopsy. However, about forty-five pictures taken during the postmortem were confiscated by federal officials. According to Wilber, these were "spirited away by presumed Secret Service agents and hidden somewhere. A roll of film exposed by a Navy enlisted technician was destroyed by some government 'agent.'"[27]

Why the photos were suppressed is a matter of conjecture. Some say it was, like the autopsy itself, handled differently out of respect for the Kennedy family's privacy. But some believe that the photos showed evidence that Kennedy was shot from the front and the back, therefore proving the existence of two shooters.

Inaccurate drawings of the bullet wounds, as shown in this autopsy report, further complicate the theories behind the assassination.

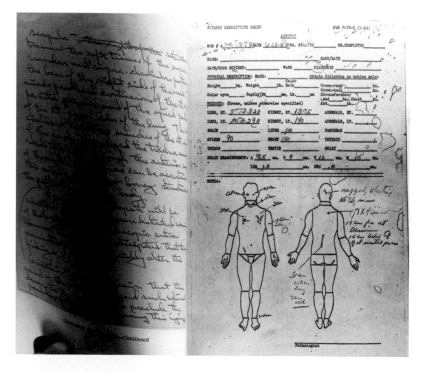

Whatever the reason, these vital investigative tools, routinely presented in any murder case, were never examined by the Warren Commission. The Assassination Records Review Board claims that this decision was made by Warren Commission member Earl Warren, who said the actual records were too graphic to be made public. Some autopsy photos and X-rays were discovered by the HSCA in later years but the nature and origin of these pictures is in dispute, and some claim they were fabricated after the autopsy.

By the Numbers

70%

Number of Americans in 1965 who believed Oswald did not act alone.

Instead of using photos to determine the cause of the president's death, the Warren Commission was given schematic drawings of his wounds. These were illustrations in pencil made by a medical corps sailor. According to Wilber,

> these schematics were based on oral instructions from Commander Humes and several of his associates. Oral descriptions only were available to the sailor who was supposed to draw a meaningful sketch of the wounds including size, location, and the like. . . . Any ordinary citizen in his right mind would know that a photograph of a wound is essential to give precise location, shape, etc. No artist's drawing, no matter how precise and exact, can reflect the nature of a wound.[28]

And, in fact, the drawings were not accurate. For example, the HSCA determined that Kennedy's back wound was drawn almost 2 inches (5cm) higher than the photos revealed. Some suggest that this means the bullet might not have come from the sixth floor of the Book Depository but rather from street level. Despite the questionable value of the schematics, the Warren Commission used them to create diagrams of the bullet trajectories as the bullets were believed to have passed through the president's head and body.

Much Mishandling of Evidence

The physical evidence generated by the autopsy was also mishandled according to critics. Under normal circumstances involving a gunshot wound of this type, the remnants of the brain would have been removed and sectioned into quarters to trace the trajectory and direction of the bullet. In addition, pathologists would look for bullet fragments in the brain that contain a microscopic "fingerprint" linked to a specific rifle,

Becoming a Medical Examiner

Job Description:
A medical examiner is a doctor who is a licensed pathologist certified to practice forensic medicine. Medical examiners conduct autopsies to examine tissue, organs, body fluids and cells in an effort to discover the cause of disease or death. Medical examiners may also evaluate blood tests, analyze DNA evidence, and assist with rape examinations.

Education:
Prospective medical examiners are required to attend four years of medical school and acquire a medical degree. Aspiring medical examiners must then complete a residency in forensic pathology for three to eight years.

Qualifications:
A medical examiner must be certified as a licensed pathologist and applicants must pass an examination given by the American Board of Pathology.

Additional Information:
The final step for becoming a medical examiner requires requesting appointment to a post by the state.

Salary:
Between $245,000 and $336,000 annually.

such as the Mannlicher-Carcano Oswald was accused of using in the assassination.

While a partial autopsy of the brain was conducted by Humes, Boswell, and Finck, the sectioning was never completed. In addition, vital materials from the case, such as microscopic tissue slides of the brain disappeared. They were sent to the National Archives in October 1966, but it was later revealed that these items had disappeared from the archives.

Many investigators argue that taken together, the missing brain evidence, the autopsy methodology, the schematic drawings, and the lack of autopsy photographs provide inconclusive evidence regarding the presidential homicide. Any competent defense lawyer would have used the numerous discrepancies in court to cast doubt about Oswald's guilt.

The motives of the government officials involved in the autopsy are a matter of conjecture. But whatever their intentions, they were remiss in their duties and that fueled speculation and rumor for decades. As respected statesman Bertrand Russell stated in 1964: "There has never been a more subversive, conspiratorial, unpatriotic, or endangering course for the United States and the world than the attempt by the United States to hide the truth behind the murder of its recent president."[29]

CHAPTER 3

The Bullets and the Gun

In the aftermath of a homicide, field analysts examine the crime scene and collect and process evidence. If possible, bullets and shrapnel fragments are gathered from the victim and crime scene in order to link the projectiles to a specific weapon. Bullet holes in the street, curb, or walls might also be analyzed to understand the trajectory of the bullets and establish the number of shots fired. If a suspect is in custody, then he or she might be given a skin test for gunshot residue. When a person fires a gun, tiny particles are expelled from the weapon and the particles, or residue, can land on a person's hands and clothes.

The study of evidence from firearms used in crimes is called forensic ballistics. By understanding the ballistics, authorities hope to create a trail of evidence linking a bullet to a weapon to the person who shot the gun. This allows a suspect to be charged with a crime.

Beyond the ballistics, a firearm can also be dusted for finger and palm prints. These prints are produced by sweat, oil, and other substances on the skin. They are invisible to the naked eye but are left on nearly every surface a person touches, including weapons and bullet casings. Because each individual has unique patterns on his or her fingers and hands, authorities can lift finger and palm prints from murder weapons and trace them to a specific suspect. This is done by dusting the prints with a dark powder and transferring the powder to special sticky tape.

Three Shots in Dallas?

When President John F. Kennedy was assassinated in Dallas, the forensic ballistics work was conducted by the Dallas Police

Department (DPD) and FBI agents. Their mission was to establish how many bullets were fired, their direction of travel, and their angle. This would allow the authorities to determine if the president was shot from above, behind, the front, or the side. It would also allow them to determine the number of shooters.

The official version of the forensic ballistics in the Kennedy case is contained in the Warren report. The Warren Commission concluded Lee Harvey Oswald fired three shots at the president from the sixth-floor window of the Texas School Book Depository. The commission based its conclusion about the number of bullets fired, in part, on the gun and the three spent shell casings found near the window on the sixth floor of the building. As an added precaution, the Warren Commission ordered tests on the gun to confirm whether it was accurate enough and could be fired quickly enough to be the murder weapon. The forensic ballistic evidence used by the Warren Commission to reconstruct the murder of the president has long been a subject of intense debate.

Critics have questioned the number of shots fired, their trajectories, the gun used, the condition of the bullets said to have caused the wounds, Oswald's ability as a marksman, and his palm print on the gun. And as with the Kennedy autopsy, there are enough mysteries, riddles, suspicions, and inexplicable actions on the part of government officials to cast doubt on several aspects the official story.

The Rifle

In any gun-related murder, the firearm purportedly used in the commission of the crime is central to the investigation. In the investigation of the Kennedy assassination, even this most basic piece of evidence, the so-called smoking gun that would prove who committed the murder, has been a subject of controversy.

By the Numbers

5.6 SECONDS

Amount of time it took Kennedy's assassin to fire the bullets that killed the president.

COMMISSION EXHIBIT
#139

This Mannlicher-Carcano rifle was found on the sixth floor of the Texas School Book Depository building after Kennedy's assassination.

The Warren report states that the murder weapon was an Italian-made, World War II–vintage, Mannlicher-Carcano, 6.5mm military rifle with a Japanese-made scope. However, when police first found a gun at the Texas School Book Depository shortly after the president was shot, these law enforcement professionals identified the rifle as a high-powered, German-made 7.65 Mauser. The rifle had one shell in the chamber and three spent shells were found nearby.

For the next twenty-four hours, the DPD reported that the murder weapon was a Mauser, and this was announced on various television and radio news reports. The weapon was also described as a Mauser in a several official DPD reports, sworn affidavits, and in a CIA report dated November 25.

About two days after the assassination, Dallas police stated that the rifle was in reality a Mannlicher-Carcano 6.5mm carbine, serial number C-2766. The discrepancy was later explained by experts who noted the Mauser and the Mannlicher-Carcano are similar in appearance. But the inconsistency causes conspiracy theorists to suspect foul play. They say the gun was switched after investigators discovered Oswald owned a Mannlicher-Carcano, not a Mauser, so they could frame Oswald for the murder.

Linking the Rifle to Oswald

The FBI announced that the Mannlicher-Carcano was traced to Klein's Sporting Goods, a mail-order operation in Chicago. The rifle and scope had been purchased on March 20, 1963, with a $21.45 money order signed by A. Hidell whose postal address was PO Box 2915, Dallas, Texas. Oswald used the alias Alek J. Hidell and the handwriting on the money order was analyzed by handwriting experts who matched it to Oswald.

The Chain of Evidence

There are many odd aspects concerning the Mannlicher-Carcano rifle traced to Oswald in the Kennedy assassination. This includes the handling of the weapon, the most important piece of evidence in the Kennedy case.

The rifle found on the sixth floor of the Texas School Book Depository after the killing was taken to a crime lab by Lieutenant J.C. Day of the crime scene search section of the Dallas Police Department. Day photographed the weapon and said he lifted a partial palm print off the barrel. This print was inconclusive but traced to Oswald nonetheless. Day did not follow standard procedures by photographing the palm print before lifting it. Further investigation was cut short because Day was ordered to give the rifle to FBI agent Vince Drain. The agent was never told of the palm print. Drain took the rifle to Washington, D.C. and gave it to Agent Robert Frazier who, for reasons unknown, kept it in his office for three days. The rifle was then sent back to Dallas for reasons unknown. Eventually the rifle was turned over to an FBI fingerprint expert in Washington, D.C. who could not find any prints on the weapon.

The manner in which the rifle was handled both in Dallas and Washington, D.C., muddied the chain of evidence. Since it was passed from person to person and not kept in a controlled environment, legal experts question whether or not the rifle could be traced to Oswald in a court of law.

Whether or not Oswald actually handled the Mannlicher-Carcano is another matter of debate. The wooden stock of the gun is rough and does not hold fingerprints. Dallas police officer J.C. Day claimed he lifted a partial palm print off a metal part of the rifle the evening of the assassination. However, some argue that the quality of the print is questionable and might not have held up as evidence in court.

There are also rumors that the print was put on the rifle after Oswald's death. Those who question the palm print evidence point to conflicting reports regarding when the palm print was supposedly discovered and when it was reported. This claim is also supported by funeral director Paul Groody, who said he was preparing Oswald's body for a memorial service when FBI agents arrived. The agents told Groody they were there to take a palm print from Oswald. This seems unusual to conspiracy theorists since finger and palm prints had been taken at the police station the day Oswald was arrested. The agents ordered the mortician to leave the room. After the agents left, Groody found ink on Oswald's palm, which had to be cleaned off. There has never been any other explanation for this visit, which was also documented at the time by reporters. Conspiracy theorists charge that while agents claimed they were taking additional prints from Oswald, they had, in fact, pushed the rifle into Oswald's hand to leave a palm print on it.

Did Oswald Fire the Rifle?

In addition to questions surrounding Oswald's handling of the rifle, some believe he never even pulled the trigger. When an individual fires a gun, in addition to leaving fingerprints, he or she will also have traces of gunpowder on the face, fingers, or clothing that can be discovered with a paraffin test. In this test, warm wax (paraffin) is applied to a suspect's skin. The paraffin opens up the pores in the skin while absorbing contaminants such as nitrates from gun powder residue. After the paraffin hardens, it is treated with a chemical that turns nitrates blue. If the wax is spotted with blue dots, it can be used as evidence in court that the suspect fired the weapon.

When Oswald was held for questioning after the assassination, he was administered a paraffin test by W.E. Barnes of the Dallas Police Department. The wax was applied to Oswald's hands and right cheek. His hands showed traces of gunpowder but his cheek did not. This meant that he could not have positioned the rifle properly to kill the president. In *Rush to Judgment* Mark Lane writes "A positive response on both hands and a negative response on the face is consistent with innocence. It is also consistent with Oswald's claim that he had not fired a rifle on November 22."[30]

Despite the negative results from Oswald's cheek, Dallas police chief Jesse Curry quickly told reporters that the paraffin test was positive and proved Oswald shot the rifle. This information was repeated by Dallas FBI agent Gordon Shanklin and reported in the *New York Times* and other major media outlets. However, at the time, the FBI's own experiments showed paraffin tests to be unreliable. And many years later, in November 2005, a study by *New Scientist* magazine proved that gunshot residue can be present in a room up to eight hours after a gun is fired and can also be picked up by suspects seated in the back seats of patrol cars. After the article was published, conspiracy theorists claimed that Oswald might have picked up the residue in the back of the patrol car after his arrest.

Did the Rifle Kill Kennedy?

In addition to the questionable evidence linking the rifle to Oswald, there is also uncertainty about the accuracy of the Mannlicher-Carcano. Some have wondered if the rifle could have been the murder weapon because of its poor quality. In *Rush to Judgment* Lane sites a 1964 article in *Mechanics Illustrated* that states the opinion that the Mannlicher-Carcano "is crudely made, poorly designed, dangerous, inaccurate . . . unreliable on repeat shots, [and] has safety design faults."[31]

The Warren report ordered several tests to determine if the Mannlicher-Carcano could have hit its mark from the Book Depository window. According to the Warren Commission, the tests showed that the gun was accurate and reliable enough to have been the murder weapon.

In one such test, FBI agents Robert Frazier, Charles Killion, and Courtland Cunningham took the rifle to a firing range on November 27, 1963, five days after Kennedy was killed. The agents took nine shots at a stationary target 15 feet (4.6m) distant. They hit the target, but the gun consistently fired high and to the right. Therefore, conspiracy theorists conclude that it is unlikely Oswald could have killed the president from his position in the sniper's nest which was 60 feet (18m) above the street. In addition, they note, Oswald was allegedly shooting at a moving target 177 to 266 feet (54m to 81m) away.

Beyond the rifle's accuracy, conspiracy theorists question whether it could actually fire three rounds in the time estimated for the shooting. Those who raise this question usually rely on a minimum estimate of 5.6 seconds for at least three shots to be fired at the president. They say that when Agent Frazier tried to shoot the Mannlicher-Carcano three times in 5.6 seconds without aiming, he was unable to do so. They point out that the Mannlicher-Carcano is a bolt-action rifle, which means that after each shot the bolt has to be pulled back to eject the spent shell and then pushed forward to place a fresh round in the chamber. The rifle would then have to be re-aimed and fired. Conspiracy theorists say Frazier could not perform this task for each bullet in less than 2.3 seconds, meaning it took this expert marksman nearly 7 seconds to fire three rounds.

In March 1964 the Warren Commission ordered the Mannlicher-Carcano retested by sharpshooters at the Infantry Weapons Evaluation Branch of the Ballistics Research Laboratory in Aberdeen, Maryland, to determine if Oswald could have fired three rounds in the time they estimated for the shooting. The difference is, the Warren Commission investigators theorized it took 5.6 seconds for the two shots that hit their mark to be fired, but they claimed all three shots may have taken up to

Oswald spent three years with the Marines and was known as a terrible shot with a rifle, scoring one point above the lowest-ranking Marine.

8 seconds. The testers were all rated as master marksmen by the National Rifle Association and all were professional gunners who conducted weapons tests for the military on a daily basis. In contrast, Oswald claimed to have barely touched a weapon since his discharge from the Marines.

In testing the weapon, the experts fired the Mannlicher-Carcano from a tower 30 feet (9m) above the ground at three stationary targets. They were placed at distances of 175, 240, and 265 feet (53m, 73m, and 81m). The men fired two series of three shots each, a total of eighteen rounds. One marksman was able to get off three shots in under 5.6 seconds. The others required 6.45 to 8.25 seconds. Based on this test, the Warren Commission believed that the rifle could have fired three rounds in the several seconds in took for president to be assassinated.

Commenting on numerous problems with this ballistics test, Lane writes:

> The Commission found that Oswald was at a sixth-floor window 60 feet above the ground but the experts fired from a tower . . . 30 feet above the ground. The Commission said that Oswald fired at a moving target but the experts fired at three stationary ones. . . . The Commission found that since the [president's] limousine was hidden by an oak tree, Oswald had less than eight-tenths of one second to take aim and fire the first shot, but the Report noted "the marksmen took as much time as they wanted for the first target." In addition to this, the rifle sight was rebuilt and two or three metal "shims" were fitted to provide a degree of accuracy previously absent. . . . Although the conditions of the test tended to diminish the difficulties . . . [not] one of them struck the enlarged head or neck on the target even once while Oswald was supposed to do it twice.[32]

According to Lane, the official ballistic tests only proved that if Oswald killed the president alone, then he could not have done it with the Mannlicher-Carcano. "Yet the [rifle] was used by the commission as proof of Oswald's guilt,"[33] on the basis of the palm print and mail-order paperwork.

The Single-Bullet Theory

Since one shot, usually assumed to be the first shot, missed the limousine's occupants, and the Warren Commission believed only three shots were fired, they had to explain how only two bullets caused nine wounds in Kennedy and Connally. The answer was provided by Arlen Specter, an assistant counselor to the Warren Commission who would later be elected a U.S. senator from Pennsylvania in 1980.

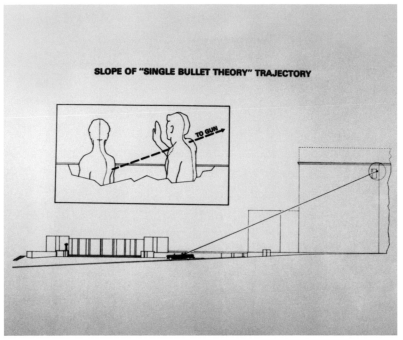

SLOPE OF "SINGLE BULLET THEORY" TRAJECTORY

The single-bullet theory by Arlen Specter states that a second shot caused eight separate non-fatal wounds in both Kennedy and Connally. Some experts do not believe that one bullet could have traveled through Kennedy's neck, Connally's back, and ricocheted to create six more wounds to the men in the open limousine.

Specter is credited with authoring the single-bullet theory, called the "magic bullet"[34] theory by Lane and other conspiracy researchers. The magic bullet was the second shot fired during the assassination. The Warren report states that this second bullet, known as Commission Exhibit 399, or CE 399, caused eight separate, nonfatal wounds in both Kennedy and Connally.

Specter describes the route of the bullet through the two men, saying that CE 399 entered Kennedy's back and exited his throat. As Kennedy clutched his throat with both hands, the bullet entered Connally at the extreme right side of his back just below the right armpit. It traveled through his chest in a downward direction and exited below his right nipple. The bullet continued on, passing through Connally's right wrist, which was on his lap, and then buried itself in his left thigh.

The single-bullet theory is controversial for several reasons. Many find it hard to believe that a single bullet traveled through fifteen layers of clothing, seven layers of skin, and about 15 inches (38cm) of human tissue in Kennedy's neck. After passing through Kennedy's neck, the commission says it passed

The Magic Bullet

James J. Humes was one of the pathologists who conducted President Kennedy's postmortem. Humes was also called before the Warren Commission to comment on the pristine condition of the so-called magic bullet that was said to have caused eight wounds in Kennedy and Connally. The following testimony, in which assistant counsel Arlen Specter questions Humes about the bullet, or Exhibit 399, is from the Warren report:

Mr. SPECTER. Now looking at that bullet, Exhibit 399, Doctor Humes, could that missile have made the wound on Governor Connally's right wrist?

Commander HUMES. I think that that is most unlikely. . . . The reason I believe it most unlikely that this missile could have inflicted either of these wounds is that this missile is basically intact; its jacket appears to me to be intact, and I do not understand how it could possibly have left fragments in either of these locations.

Mr. SPECTER. Dr. Humes, under your opinion which you have just given us, what effect, if any, would that have on whether this bullet, 399, could have been the one to lodge in Governor Connally's thigh?

Commander HUMES. I think that extremely unlikely. The reports from Parkland [Memorial Hospital] tell of an entrance wound on the lower midthigh of the Governor, and X-rays taken there are described as showing metallic fragments in the bone, which apparently by this report were not removed and are still present in Governor Connally's thigh. I can't conceive of [how] they came from this missile.

Quoted in "Governor Connally's Wrist Wound and CE-399," JFK Assassination Research, November 2007, www.jfk-info.com/fragment.htm.

through the president's necktie knot, entered Connally and removed 4 inches (10cm) of his rib before passing through the front of Connally's midsection and shattering the radius bone in his wrist.

According to the Warren report, the bullet that did this damage was recovered from the stretcher used to wheel Connally into the operating room on the second floor of Parkland Memorial Hospital. After the governor was placed on an operating table, the stretcher was wheeled into an elevator and traveled to the ground floor unattended. It was then removed from the elevator by senior hospital engineer Darrell C. Tomlinson, who wheeled the stretcher into the hallway and pushed it up against another stretcher unrelated to the assassination. At that time, the bullet rolled off onto the floor and was discovered by Tomlinson and given to nearby Secret Service agents Richard Johnson and Bill Greer. Both men were guarding Trauma Room One where doctors were fighting to save President Kennedy.

There are controversies surrounding the discovery of this bullet, however. Some say the bullet did not come from the stretcher; it came from Trauma Room One. This is taken to mean that CE 399 fell out of the wound in the president's back and could not have been the bullet that wounded Connally. If that is true, then four or more shots were fired that day, the first missed, two hit Kennedy, and at least one hit the governor.

> **By the Numbers**
>
> **8**
>
> **Number of wounds allegedly caused by a single bullet fired from Oswald's gun.**

Was the Bullet Pristine?

Those who believe in the four-shot theory point to the condition of the magic bullet. As seen in the Warren report, CE 399 was pristine, that is, visibly perfect, not compacted or damaged. According to the testimony of ballistic experts who appeared before the Warren Commission, any bullet that passed through the bone and tissue of two people would be flattened, distorted, and broken apart. As Irving Shaw, a former army surgeon who

It is unknown whether this bullet came from Governor Connally's stretcher or President Kennedy's. The photo, Exhibit 399 of the Warren Commission, shows a clean bullet which suggests it did not come into contact with either body.

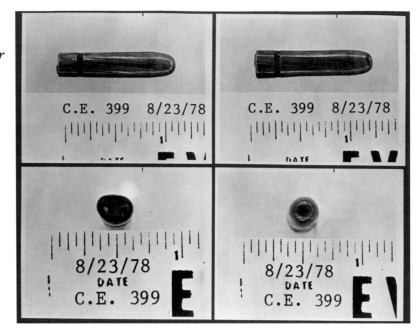

had treated over one thousand gunshot wounds, told Spector, "I feel that there would be some difficulty in explaining all of the wounds as being inflicted by bullet Exhibit 399 without causing more in the way of loss of substance to the bullet or deformation of the bullet."[35]

Although many conspiracy theories were built on the condition of the magic bullet, in later years, experts contradicted Shaw's testimony. From 1976 to 1977, the House Select Committee on Assassinations (HSCA) addressed the pristine bullet issue. They noted that the bullet is steel jacketed, that is, the soft lead bullet is plated with a thin layer of steel in order to travel at a higher velocity. Therefore, CE 399 could have caused the eight wounds without becoming distorted or broken. As the HSCA report states, the bullet is a "long, stable, fully jacketed bullet, typical of ammunition often used by the military. Such ammunition tends to pass through body tissue more easily than soft nose hunting bullets [while still maintaining their original shape]."[36] Although there was no blood, human tissue, or clothing fibers on the bullet, supporters of the Warren Commission believe that the steel jacket allowed the bullet to penetrate both men.

"Not Conclusive"

Whatever the makeup of the bullet, critics contend that a single projectile could not have inflicted the wounds doctors observed in the two men. The bullet, they contend, would have had to change course several times and move in a manner that defies physics and logic. To create these wounds critics say, CE 399 would have had to exit Kennedy's neck, stop in midair, turn to the right, move over 18 inches (46cm), stop again, and then

The position of Kennedy and Connally in the limousine leaves much room for debate of bullet trajectories. Connally was sitting to the left of Kennedy and was turned at a different angle, which disputes the single-bullet theory.

continue on its way through Connally's back. After exiting Connally's body, CE 399 would have had to move downward, go through the right wrist and somehow jog over from his right wrist to his left thigh.

Supporters of the single-bullet theory point out, however, that Connally was not sitting directly in front of Kennedy nor was he at the same height. Connally was sitting in a jump seat that was

What the Witnesses Say

There were at least 260 witnesses to Kennedy's assassination standing in Dealey Plaza that day. Although eyewitness testimony is often deemed unreliable, researchers have used it to bolster their contention that there was a conspiracy.

Part of the problem is that the Warren Commission ignored testimony from forty witnesses who contradicted the lone gunman theory put forth in the Warren report. These people testified that the shot that killed Kennedy came from the front. Typical of these witnesses is observer Jean Hill who stated: "I saw a man fire from behind the wooden fence. I saw a puff of smoke and some sort of movement from the grassy knoll." County surveyor Robert West, whose job required him to carefully scrutinize land boundaries, said the shots came "from the northwest quadrant of Dealey Plaza—the area of the picket fence on the grassy knoll." A retired air force major, who knew about weapons and gunshots, said "I saw blood going to the rear and left. . . . That doesn't happen if the bullet came from the Depository." Others support the theory that shots were also fired from the Texas School Book Depository, but not from the sixth-floor sniper's nest. Factory worker Carolyn Walther said: "I glanced up at the Depository Building. There were two men in the corner window on the fourth or fifth floor. One man . . . held a rifle with the barrel pointed downward [at Kennedy]. I thought he was some kind of guard."

Quoted in Richard Belzer, *UFOs, JFK,* and *Elvis.* New York: Ballantine, 1999, p. 42.

lower and to the president's left. And the governor was turned at an angle, waving to people. The Warren Commission recreated the scene with models in a similar limousine, and in 1988 the PBS show *Nova* used computer animation to test the theory. Based on photographs from that day, these reconstructions of the crime had Kennedy leaning uncomfortably forward at a 25-degree angle when he was first shot. This would have allowed a bullet to enter his back and exit his lower neck and hit Connally. However, no photos show Kennedy sitting at this angle and so debate continues over the exact positions of the two men, the physics of the bullet, the effects of bone and clothing on its trajectory, and the blurry photographic evidence used as a basis for the tests. Adding doubt are the words in the Warren report which state the bullet "most probably" passed through the two men and "the alignment of the points of entry was only indicative and not conclusive that one bullet hit both men. The exact positions of the men could not be re-created; thus, the angle could only be approximated."[37]

The Shot That Missed

The magic bullet is not the only shot creating controversy. The Warren Commission says that one shot missed the limousine completely and hit the south curb of Main Street, wounding bystander James Tague slightly in the cheek. Immediately after the assassination, Deputy Buddy Walthers examined the ground nearby for bullets. Walthers initially claimed that he found this bullet lying in the grass and handed it to a man he believed to be an FBI agent. This man pocketed the bullet and it was never seen again. However, Walthers later changed his story, saying he never found a bullet but instead discovered a piece of Kennedy's skull, which he gave the agent.

In another twist, the curb was exposed to the elements for nine months before the city dug it up and sent it to the FBI so the groove in the cement could at be matched to the same type of bullet used by the Mannlicher-Carcano. When conspiracy researchers later asked to see the curb, the agency told them that this evidence had been thrown away.

At least two more bullet marks were allegedly found in streets around the murder scene. These bullet marks also have a curious history. According to conspiracy researchers, the bullet trajectory on a man-hole cover in Dealey Plaza lines up perfectly with the Dallas Records Building on Houston Street where another assassin might have been stationed. Another bullet hit the limousine on the window frame above the rearview mirror. Theorists say this came from almost straight behind the limousine, most likely from the second floor of the Dal-Tex Building. If all of these shots were truly fired then there must have been at least two assassins at work in Dealey Plaza—and maybe more. But there has never been definitive proof to contradict the Warren report, which says three shots were fired from the Texas School Book Depository. At this time, the forensic ballistics in the Kennedy assassination remain a matter of debate.

CHAPTER 4

Audio Forensics and Evidence on Film

When President John F. Kennedy was assassinated in 1963, the media world was primitive by modern standards. Compared to the high-tech, globally linked, digital media of today, the technical abilities of reporters were severely limited. They had pencils and pads, reel-to-reel tape recorders the size of small suitcases, 35mm film cameras, and clunky 16mm movie cameras. Film required processing and editing before it could be broadcast. Television cameras were huge, required massive amounts of electricity, and had to be warmed up for two hours before they were "hot" enough for use. They could not be removed from studios. Breaking news was generally transmitted to newspapers and television stations by reporters using pay phones.

As Kennedy's limousine slowly wound its way through the streets of Dallas, there were no radio or television stations broadcasting the event. On most occasions, press photographers rode on a flatbed truck in front of the presidential limousine so that camera crews could snap pictures and film the president from a clear angle as he waved to the crowds. On November 22, however, Kennedy's motorcade was not deemed important enough news to warrant such coverage. Most camera operators were waiting at the Dallas Trade Mart, ready to cover the president's speech.

There was a press pool car in the motorcade. It was a borrowed telephone company vehicle equipped with a mobile radio telephone, primitive mobile-phone technology that broadcast over radio waves. Riders in the press pool car included Merriman Smith, United Press International's White House reporter; Malcolm Kilduff, acting White House press secretary; and three other reporters with cameras wedged in the back seat. Secret Service agents inexplicably put the press vehicle five cars

One Journalist's Report

In 1963 Merriman Smith, a veteran reporter with United Press International and assigned to the White House, was on the scene in Dallas when President Kennedy was assassinated. Although he was 150 to 200 yards (137m to 183m) behind the president's limousine when the shooting started, his is the only eyewitness report from a professional journalist. Smith's article appeared in newspapers the day after Kennedy's death. He writes:

I was riding in the so-called White House press "pool" car. . . . Suddenly we heard three loud, almost painful loud cracks. The first sounded as if it might have been a large firecracker, but the second and third blasts were unmistakable. Gunfire.

One sees history explode before one's eyes and for even the most trained observer, there is a limit to what one can comprehend. . . .

Everyone in our car began shouting at the driver to pull up closer to the President's car, but at this moment, we saw the big [limousine] and a motorcycle escort roar away at high speed.

We screamed at our driver, "Get going, get going." We . . . set out down the highway, barely able to keep in sight of the President's car. . . . They vanished around a curve. When we cleared the same curve we could see where we were heading—Parkland Hospital . . . I ran to the side of the [car].

The President was face down on the back seat. Mrs. Kennedy made a cradle of her arms around the President's head and bent over him as if she were whispering to him.

Merriman Smith, "Eyewitness: The Death of President Kennedy," United Press International, November 23, 1963, www.downhold.org/lowry/kennedy.html.

behind the president. Why this happened remains a mystery. Smith reported that he was 150 to 200 yards (137m to 183m) behind Kennedy's car when the shooting started.

Without reporters nearby, there is a very limited number of auditory or visual records of Kennedy being shot. One sound recording, some amateur films, and photos were created. They have been studied extensively by forensic experts who specialize in photography and audio analysis. But the experts have come to many different conclusions.

The Dictabelt Recording

One of the most pressing questions in the Kennedy assassination is how many shots were fired that day. If there was more than three, then it is likely there was more than one shooter and the conclusions in the Warren report are wrong. An audio tape of the assassination would have quickly solved the mystery. Unfortunately, the only sound recording available provides no conclusive answer.

During the era when Kennedy was shot, police departments recorded radio communications on a machine called a Dictaphone. This dictation machine recorded sounds in grooves pressed into a thin celluloid belt, called a Dictabelt. By chance, there was a Dictabelt recording made around the time Kennedy's motorcade was driving through Dealey Plaza. A motorcycle policeman accidentally left the microphone on

The only sound recording taken during the time of Kennedy's assassination was from a police officer's Dictabelt—a dictation machine worn on the officer's belt. Although the recording is five minutes long, it is still unclear how many shots were fired.

his police radio "open" or on, for about five and a half minutes, blocking out all other police calls on the Dictabelt.

Difficult Audio Analysis

Although the recording was not addressed by the Warren Commission, its existence was revealed to the House Select Committee on Assassinations (HSCA) in 1979. The committee hired James Barger to analyze the tape. Barger was an expert in audio forensics and chief scientist for BBN Technologies, a company that was developing Internet communications technology at that time.

The tape Barger analyzed does not contain the distinctive sound of rifle shots but rather static noise mixed with distant voices. In order to hear the rifle shots, Barger used a computer technique called adaptive filtering. This technique allowed him to subtract the sound of the motorcycle engine, which was the loudest noise the tape. However, even after applying adaptive filtering, it was still impossible to hear audible shots. But Barger saw five electrical impulses on his computer printout that he believed to be the shots.

To investigate further, Barger used a technique called matched filtering, a method to detect barely audible sounds on the Dictabelt. To apply match filtering, he needed to match the sound waves on the printout to a clear audio record of rifle fire in Dealey Plaza. This would require a complicated test. In order to convince the HSCA to pay for it, he presented the committee with a graph of the audio impulses on a roll of paper 23 feet (7m) long.

Until this time the HSCA had not been able to disprove the conclusions of the Warren report. With Barger's news, committee members were galvanized. On August 20, 1978, at the direction of the congressional committee, the Dallas Police Department closed Dealey Plaza to the public. Marksmen, using a Mannlicher-Carcano rifle like Oswald's, shot fifty-seven bullets into piles of sandbags in the middle of the street. The shots were recorded by Barger and a team of audio scientists using a series of microphones placed along the path of the 1963 motorcade. The scientists then used the audio records to make a series of 2,592 calculations involving 432 combinations of rifle shots and microphone locations. This provided them with a pattern of sound waves called an "acoustic fingerprint" that could be read like a map and matched to the electrical impulses on the Dictabelt recording.

One Expert's Conclusion

Barger came to the final conclusion that four shots were fired when Kennedy was killed. According to his testimony, there was better than an 88 percent chance that three of the shots came from the direction of the Texas School Book Depository. The fourth shot came from the grassy knoll in front of JFK's limousine. According to Bob Callahan in *Who Shot JFK?*,

the grassy knoll shot was there all right. From its [acoustic] fingerprint, the scientists were able to deduce within a margin of error . . . one and a half feet the exact location of the microphone which had recorded the shot. . . . [Barger] then reached an even

Lost television footage taken during the Kennedy assassination shows law officers and witnesses ran to the rail yard behind the Texas School Book Depository to search for the assassin after shots were fired.

71

more astounding conclusion. The acoustic fingerprint located the grassy knoll gunman within a margin of error of plus or minus five feet in circumference at the exact point behind the wooden fence where Lee Bowers [who worked in a nearby railroad switching tower] had once seen an unidentified man standing . . . [and] had seen a puff of smoke rise in the seconds after the actual shooting. There was at least one additional shooter working from behind the fence.[38]

As a result of the audio forensics, the HSCA announced in its final report in March 1979 that Kennedy was "probably assassinated as a result of conspiracy."[39] The committee agreed with the Warren report that Oswald fired three shots from the Book Depository. But taking their conclusions entirely from Barger's findings, the HSCA report states that there was a high probability that a second gunman shot at, but missed, Kennedy. Although the committee members could not positively identify the coconspirators, the chief counsel and staff director of the committee, G. Robert Blakey, said "I am now firmly of the opinion that the Mob did it."[40]

Blakey's Bias

To no one's surprise, there was vociferous disagreement over the HSCA conclusions. Law enforcement experts who studied the Mafia concluded that Kennedy's murder did not bear any of the classic signs of a mob hit. The Mafia had a record of never killing public officials, so it was seen as unlikely that they would murder the most visible public official on Earth. In addition, despite a few high-profile hits in public places, most professional Mafia gunmen made sure there were no witnesses, let alone thousands of people watching a public event like a presidential motorcade.

Whether or not Blakey's Mafia assertion is true, his conspiracy conclusions were soon called into question because he had said: "If the acoustics come out that we made a mistake somewhere, I think that would end it."[41]

Another Analysis, Another Conclusion

As it turned out, a musician and amateur acoustic researcher named Steve Barber came to the conclusion that the acoustics were wrong. After listening to a copy of the Dictabelt recording for four months, Barber was able to pick out the voice of Sheriff Bill Decker saying "hold everything secure"[42] in the exact place on the recording where the shots purportedly occurred. However, Decker is known to have uttered those words about one minute after Kennedy was shot. This means that the Dictabelt in question was recorded after the shots were fired.

Barber contacted the FBI, Dallas police, and the National Academy of Sciences (NAS) with his evidence. After a lengthy study, the NAS confirmed Barber's conclusions. The tape was made after Kennedy was shot. However, conspiracy theorists came to their own conclusions. Some believed Decker's voice had been deliberately added to the recording after the fact to confuse the truth. Others said that the Dictabelt recording head was bumped during the recording and the needle recorded over the same spot twice. However, the NAS tested for these possibilities and concluded "reliable acoustic data do not support a conclusion that there was a second gunman."[43]

> **By the Numbers**
>
> # 26 SECONDS
>
> **Length of the Zapruder film showing Kennedy's assassination.**

The Zapruder Film: An Unimpeachable Record?

Audio forensic experts investigating the Kennedy assassination arrived at two contradictory conclusions. But the most famous filmed record of the event has generated dozens of conflicting theories and has spawned books, movies, and countless articles.

The film of the Kennedy assassination was not made by a professional camera operator. It was shot by Abraham Zapruder, a woman's clothing manufacturer from New York City who was

Bystander Abraham Zapruder's 8mm film footage of Kennedy's assassination generated conflicting theories about the event.

PHOTOGRAPH FROM ZAPRUDER FILM

PHOTOGRAPH FROM RE-ENACTMENT

PHOTOGRAPH THROUGH RIFLE SCOPE

DISTANCE TO STATION C	181.9 FT.
DISTANCE TO RIFLE IN WINDOW	218.0 FT.
ANGLE TO RIFLE IN WINDOW	18°03'
DISTANCE TO OVERPASS	307.1 FT.
ANGLE TO OVERPASS	+0°44'

FRAME 255

living in Dallas on the day of the murder. Zapruder's office was in the Dal-Tex Building, directly across the street from the Texas School Book Depository. As a staunch supporter of the president, Zapruder decided to take time off work to watch Kennedy's motorcade pass through Dealey Plaza. Although he was simply planning to observe the event, he made a fateful decision and went home first to get his Bell and Howell Zoomatic 8mm movie camera so he could film the president as he passed.

Zapruder was filming as shots rang out and the president was murdered. Incredibly, his 26 seconds of grainy color film are the only clear photographic record of Kennedy's murder. As *Life* magazine describes it, "of all the witnesses to the tragedy, the only unimpeachable one is the 8-mm movie camera of Abraham Zapruder."[44]

Unfortunately, each frame of an 8mm film is less than one-third of an inch square, so enlargements made from the tiny frames are low quality. And Zapruder's camera did not have audio capabilities to record sound. This left investigators wondering if the film could help them discover exactly how many shots were fired and at what intervals they occurred. Because the camera shot 18.3 frames of film per second (with each frame representing 1/18.3 of a second) the twenty-six seconds of film yielded 488.8 frames in all. Of those, approximately 105 frames capture the president being struck by two bullets, one striking him in the neck and the other hitting his head.

Forensic photographers have been able to use these individual frames as a "clock" and determine the sequence of events by looking at each individual frame. For example, the Warren Commission divided 105 frames by 18.8, and determined that the assassination took place in about 5.6 seconds.

How Many Shots Were Filmed?

While the Zapruder film provides important information, it does not tell the complete story of the assassination. For example, Kennedy's limousine passes behind a freeway sign at frame 210 and emerges at frame 225. At this time, Kennedy is already grabbing his throat with both hands, his reaction to being shot. This left the Warren Commission to conclude "the President was probably shot through the neck between frames 210 and 225."[45]

If the Warren Commission had stopped there, the matter of when the president was shot might have been settled. But the commission muddled its own conclusion when it added that "a victim of a bullet wound may not react immediately and, in some situations . . . the victim may not even know where he has been hit, or when."[46] This indicates that Kennedy may have been reacting to a shot fired before frame 210.

The Warren Commission believed, based on witness testimony and bullet casings found in the Book Depository that three shots were fired at the president's limousine that day. As it examined the Zapruder film, the commission looked for the timing of these three shots. Some people viewed the film evidence and came to different conclusions. Conspiracy researchers say the film shows as many as six shots were fired that day in Dealey Plaza.

Most theories state that frame 150 of the film shows the president turning to his right and looking at the grassy knoll. At this point the Warren Commission says Kennedy is reacting to

An aerial view of Kennedy's route through Dallas. Experts looking at the Zapruder footage say the second shot may have come from the triple underpass, shown in the forefront.

The Hidden Zapruder Film

With so many questions concerning the Kennedy assassination, even a photographic record is not enough to silence the critics of the Warren report. This stems from the strange and curious events surrounding the Zapruder film, the clearest known record of the murder.

After the assassination, Abraham Zapruder had at least three copies made of the film. He gave one print to the Dallas FBI and one to Secret Service agents who flew it to Washington, D.C. to be analyzed by the National Photographic Interpretations Center, where many copies were made and given to the CIA and other agencies. Zapruder sold one copy to *Life* magazine for $250,000. Although several still frames of the film were published in the magazine, the editors did not print frames 314 to 320 that purport to show the president's backward motion at the fatal head shot.

Life bought the rights to the film and kept it out of the public for twelve years. Americans never got to see the actual movie of Kennedy's murder until 1975. When photographic expert Robert J. Groden finally analyzed the film, he saw what appears to be a shot to the president's head from the front which would have cast serious doubt on the conclusions of the Warren report.

the first shot fired, the one that missed the car. Critics say that Oswald would not have fired when the president's limo was in that location because an oak tree would have blocked the view of anyone in the sniper's nest on the sixth floor of the Book Depository. There is little doubt, however, that the first shot was fired at this time because it so startled Zapruder that his hand involuntarily jerked in reaction, blurring the images in the film.

The president continued to wave until shot number two pierced his throat. Although the Warren Commission says the second shot was fired by Oswald from behind the president, critics say frames 188 through 191 of the Zapruder film seem to show the president's body pushed backward by the force of the bullet. They contend that this proves shot two came from the front, either from the grassy knoll or the top of the Triple Underpass. At this point, the limousine disappears from view behind a highway sign, but when it emerges on frame 225, the president is clearly clutching his throat with both hands.

A third shot, say conspiracy researchers, was fired at almost the same time as the second. This missed Kennedy and hit Connally in the chest. The Zapruder film shows Connally clearly holding his white Stetson cowboy hat in his right hand. Some who have studied the film claim that it would have been impossible for the governor to hang onto his hat if he was also shot through the wrist by this bullet, as the single-bullet theory proposes. Others say it would not be unusual for the governor to continue gripping his hat in reflex.

Theorists also claim the alleged third shot did not come from the sixth-floor sniper nest in the Book Depository but from the opposite end of the building on fourth or fifth floor. Shot four is said to have struck Kennedy in the middle of his back, 6 inches (15cm) below the shoulder. This bullet might have been fired from a second-floor window of the Dal-Tex Building.

Shot from the Grassy Knoll?

The shot that killed the president is clearly shown on frame 313, hitting him in the right temple and leaving a hole the size of a fist in his head. This shot has also generated its share of controversy. According to common conspiracy theories, this fatal blow was the fifth shot fired that day, not the third as the Warren Commission report contends. Some researchers also contend that the Zapruder film clearly shows Kennedy's body thrown back and to the left as if the shot came from the front right—which would be the grassy knoll.

When the HSCA looked into this issue, it reached conflicting conclusions. Michael Baden, head of the committee's forensic pathology panel concluded that "nerve damage from a bullet entering [the front of] the President's head could have caused his back muscles to tighten which, in turn, could have caused his head to move toward the rear . . . [and] the rearward movement of the President's head would not be fundamentally inconsistent with a bullet striking from the rear."[47] Others disagree, however, and this issue has never been resolved. But as Gary L. Aguilar writes in *Murder in Dealey Plaza*, "any bullet striking JFK at the base of his skull from Oswald's supposed perch would have created a 'blow-out' exit wound in JFK's face. . . . Including a good portion of the right forehead, the entire right eye socket, and part of the cheekbone."[48] The president did not have this sort of wound.

Those who believe that there were two shooters also say that a sixth shot is alleged to have come about a half-second later. Shot six, said to be fired from the same window in the Book Depository as number three, hit Connally, shattering his right wrist and exiting into his thigh. The governor reacted to this shot by dropping his Stetson hat.

If all these shots were fired, as conspiracy theorists say, then there must have been at least two assassins at work in Dealey Plaza—and maybe more. And none of the shots seem to have come from Oswald's sniper's nest in the Book Depository.

An Inside Job?

Some take the theory of two assassins even further and make the shocking claim that Secret Service agents were in on the plot to kill the president. To support this unproved claim, they point to the inaction of the agents even as shots rained down on the motorcade. In *UFOs, JFK, and Elvis*, Warren report critic Richard Belzer writes:

> As researchers have documented . . . photos taken at
> the time of the shooting show a bizarre lack of reaction
> from the agents riding behind Kennedy. While the

president grasps his throat, Secret Service agents are looking around—two toward the rear and two toward Kennedy. With the exception of Clint Hill, an agent brought in at the last minute by the First Lady, they make no move to shield the president from further gunfire. Most peculiar, after the first shot is fired, Kennedy's driver, Secret Service Agent William Greer, actually brings the car to a halt. Though he testified that he kept the Lincoln moving between twelve and fifteen miles per hour at all times, [the Zapruder film] clearly show the car slowing to nearly a standstill until the fatal bullet hits its mark.[49]

Zapruder's film of Kennedy's murder has become one of the most studied pieces of film in history. It was an essential part of the Warren Commission hearings. But to confuse matters further, there are some who believe that even this one vital piece of photographic evidence is fake. To support their theory, they follow the chain of possession from Zapruder to the FBI.

After the assassination, Abraham Zapruder had three or more copies made of the film—the actual number is unclear. Conspiracy theorists suggest that the Secret Service was in possession of the original print of the film for about eighteen hours after it was developed, and that it was altered, with images resized, frames removed, important details erased, and the film speed joggled. Some who claim to have seen the original say that blood and brains can be seen coming out of the back of Kennedy's head with the fatal shot, which would indicate a shot from the front. This is not seen in other prints of the film.

Other Photographic Evidence

In addition to the Zapruder film, there are several important photographic records of the assassination that are just as controversial. Mysteriously, there are also people who claim to have filmed the event only to have their work destroyed or confiscated.

Polaroid photo taken by spectator Moorman seconds before John F. Kennedy was shot in Dallas, Texas, November 22, 1963.

Beverly Oliver, a nightclub singer, claims she was standing on the other side of the street from the picket fence when Kennedy was shot. She says she filmed the scene with a brand-new movie camera and had a clear view of the grassy knoll. Oliver says she saw Kennedy's head shot and saw a figure and a puff of smoke from behind the picket fence. After the assassination, Oliver claims the FBI contacted her at work and took her film which was never seen again. However, some doubt Oliver's claims. She did not come forward until 1970 and some of her claims about the events surrounding the assassination have been disproved.

Like Oliver, another questionable witness claims to have filmed the assassination. A young serviceman named Gordon Arnold, claims he was shooting a home movie of the president from the grassy knoll with his back to the picket fence. Arnold, who had just finished live-fire training exercises in the military says he was startled to hear and feel a bullet whiz by his head from behind. Arnold says he quickly dropped to the ground as a second shot passed directly over him. After this shot found its target, a man in a policeman's uniform, but with dirty hands and no hat,

Oswald's Backyard Photographs

After Lee Harvey Oswald was taken into custody, Dallas police said they found several mysterious photographs at Oswald's home. The pictures show Oswald posing as a revolutionary, standing in the backyard with a pistol on his hip, holding a rifle in one hand, and two procommunist newspapers in the other. These photos were leaked to the press by authorities and one of them appeared on the cover of *Life* magazine on February 21, 1964. Some believe this was done to persuade the public that Oswald was guilty.

Oswald was shown these photographs after his arrest, and he claimed they were faked by a photographic expert. He said "That picture is not mine, but the face is mine. The picture has been made by superimposing my face. The other part of the picture is not me at all."

After Oswald's death, assassination researchers studied the backyard photos extensively. Some found oddities concerning the shadows in the pictures. For example, there is a dark shadow under Oswald's nose, meaning the sun was directly overhead at around noon when the picture was taken. But Oswald's neck is dark on one side and light on the other, indicating that this part of the photo was taken at 10:00 A.M. when the sun was to the side. The shadow of his body extends far out behind the person in the photo and experts say this is a 4:00 P.M. shadow. Therefore, the photos appear to be pasted together from other pictures.

Quoted in Trivia-Library.com, "JFK Assassination Last Words of Lee Harvey Oswald Part 7," Trivia-Library.com, www.trivia-library.com/b/jfk-assassination-last-words-of-lee-harvey-oswald-part-7.htm.

approached the young soldier. Arnold states that the policeman was shaking and crying and holding a rifle in his hand. This man purportedly kicked Arnold, grabbed his camera, yanked out the film, and threw it on the ground. Arnold's story has been disputed because he is not visible in any photographs taken of the scene, and he has told several different versions of the story.

Mary Ann Moorman, however, can prove she was in Dealey Plaza when the president was killed. Moorman was standing across the street from the grassy knoll and managed to click a Polaroid picture one-sixth of a second before Kennedy's fatal head shot. In 1995 photographic researchers studying the photograph claimed they could see the man dressed as a policeman mentioned by Arnold. Known as "Badgeman" because of the police badge on his chest, this grainy figure appears to be holding a rifle—and a puff of smoke is seen coming out of the barrel. Conspiracy theorists speculate that Badgeman fired the fatal shot that killed Kennedy and was dressed as a policeman in order to blend into the crowd.

This barely visible figure, blown up from a piece of photographic film less than one-tenth of an inch square, is open to interpretation. People tend to see what they want to see in these grainy images taken in an era before digital photography. This leaves forensic photographers with a crude, inconclusive record of a shocking crime.

CHAPTER 5

The Mind of Oswald

Lee Harvey Oswald, the prime suspect in Kennedy's assassination, was himself murdered before he could face a judge and jury of his peers. Because Oswald was murdered before he stood trial, historians and forensic psychologists have been left to argue his guilt or innocence based on his behavior before the murder.

Forensic psychologists combine careers in law and psychology and testify in thousands of trials. Their job, according to forensic psychologists Charles Patrick Ewing and Joseph T. McCann is to "get inside the head of a person"[50] who is involved in a criminal trial. In doing so, they determine what an individual's state of mind was when he or she participated in the event that led to his or her arrest.

While forensics psychology is less scientific than crime scene analysis, it has affected the outcome of countless trials. One notable example is the trial of John W. Hinckley Jr., who shot and wounded President Ronald Reagan and three others in March 1981 in front of dozens of witnesses. Hinckley's lawyers hired forensic psychologists in their efforts to defend Hinckley and save him from the death penalty. After psychiatric examinations, forensic psychologists determined that Hinckley was delusional. He said he shot Reagan to win the love of actress Jodie Foster. Therefore, according to the psychiatric reports, Hinckley was unable to appreciate the wrongfulness of his conduct. As a result, he was found not guilty by reason of insanity and confined for life to St. Elizabeth's psychiatric hospital in Washington, D.C.

It is possible that psychiatric forensics would have also been used in a trial for Lee Harvey Oswald. As the Warren report states, the commission was unable to reach any definitive conclusion as to whether or not Oswald "would have been judged 'sane' under prevailing legal standards. . . . [No] forum could properly make that determination unless Oswald were before it."[51]

With Oswald's death, the public is left to speculate whether he was a cold-blooded assassin, a psychotic loner seeking attention, or a hapless victim set up to look like a patsy. Whatever the case, conspiracy researchers and government authorities alike agree that Oswald had mental health issues and was emotionally unstable in the years before his death.

A Detached, Solitary Existence

Lee Harvey Oswald was born in New Orleans on October 18, 1939, two months after his father died suddenly of a heart attack. He was intelligent and studied subjects such as astronomy and astrology at a very young age. However, his intellect did not result in good grades in school. Speaking as if he was still alive, his mother, Marguerite Oswald, told the Warren Commission, "Lee has wisdom without education. From a very small child . . . Lee seemed to know the answer to things without schooling. That type of child, in a way, is bored with schooling because he is a little advanced. . . . Lee read history books, books too deep for a child that age."[52]

When Lee was around six, his mother married an engineer named Edwin A. Ekdahl who was nearly twenty years her senior. Lee took to Ekdahl right away, as Oswald's half-brother John Pic told the Warren Commission, "I think Lee found in him the father he never had. He treated us real good."[53] However, the marriage did not last long and when Oswald was nine, his mother divorced. Although Oswald was asked to testify at the divorce trial, he refused, saying that he could not tell the difference between the truth and a lie.

After the divorce, Marguerite often left Lee on his own while Pic and Lee's older brother Robert Oswald lived at the orphanage. He got up every morning, got dressed, ate,

Lee Harvey Oswald, pictured at age 8, had an unstable childhood with his mother Marguerite, who often left young Oswald home alone.

and went to go to school alone. After school, he waited in an empty house until she returned. Neighbors testified to the Warren Commission that during this period Marguerite was overbearing, while Lee was quick to anger. It was also revealed that due to their unusually close relationship, mother and son shared the same bed until Lee reached the age of eleven.

Because of his mother's poverty, they moved twenty-two times before Oswald was eighteen years old and he attended twelve different schools. They mostly lived in New Orleans and Dallas but when Oswald was thirteen, they moved to New York City to stay with Oswald's brother John Pic, who had joined the Coast Guard and was stationed there. Oswald was moody and withdrawn, possibly because of his feelings of alienation at school. As a Southern boy, his manner of dress and speech brought him unwanted attention from bullies and he

Oswald's Drawings

When Lee Harvey Oswald was undergoing psychological evaluation at the Youth House in 1953, he was given a test involving human figure drawing. Oswald was asked to draw several pictures, each featuring an individual of his choice. The results were analyzed by psychiatrist Irving Sokolow who wrote that Oswald's drawings were "empty, poor characterizations of persons approximately the same age. . . . They reflect a considerable amount of impoverishment in the social and emotional areas. . . . [Oswald] appears slightly withdrawn and in view of the lack of details in his drawings this may assume . . . some difficulty in relationships to [his mother]."

The drawing test administered by Sokolow was very popular in the 1950s because subjects could create a wide variety of pictures that were believed to reveal his or her mental state. The drawings were also used by psychological forensic experts in court. Today, however, the test is considered unreliable because there is no set standard to evaluate the patient's drawings. In Oswald's case, it is known through interviews with friends and family that he had extreme difficulty relating to others, which confirms Sokolow's diagnosis.

Quoted in Charles Patrick Ewing and Joseph T. McCann, *Minds on Trial: Great Cases in Law and Psychology*. New York: Oxford University Press, 2006, p. 25.

By the Numbers

22

Number of times Lee Harvey Oswald moved before he was eighteen.

was often harassed by other students. Rather than fight back, Oswald cut classes, spending most of his days at the Bronx Zoo studying the animals. During this period, Oswald was prone to emotional outbursts and at one point he threatened to stab Pic's wife with a small pocketknife.

The truancy problem soon became critical when Oswald missed thirty-two out of forty-seven days of class. The school recommended that Marguerite take her son to a psychiatrist, but Oswald refused to go, saying he would not visit what he called a "head shrinker or nut doctor."[54] However, in 1953 the school forced Oswald to appear before a judge in juvenile court and he was ordered to live in a residential facility for psychiatric evaluation called the Youth House. There he was interviewed by psychiatric social worker Evelyn Strickman, who took a special interest in him. She writes in a report:

> What is really surprising is that this boy has not lost entirely his ability to communicate with other people because he has been leading such a detached, solitary existence for most of his life. . . . [He] feels almost as if there is a veil between him and other people through which they cannot reach him. . . . He acknowledges fantasies about being all-powerful and being able to do anything he wanted. When I asked if this ever involved hurting or killing people, he said that it did.[55]

Another psychiatrist, Renatus Hartogs, diagnosed Oswald as having a "personality pattern disturbance with schizoid features and passive-aggressive tendencies."[56]

A schizoid personality disorder is defined as a mental illness in which a person shows a lack of interest in social relationships and a preference for a solitary lifestyle. Other symptoms include secretiveness and emotional coldness. People who exhibit passive-aggressive behavior deal with their responsibilities by acting stubborn, resentful, sullen, or helpless. According to Ewing and McCann, "individuals with this disturbance are extremely introverted and shy but are prone to intense outbursts of anger and rage. . . . [As a result] Hartogs concluded that Oswald was potentially dangerous to other people and had a [tendency] to act out explosively and aggressively."[57]

Whatever Oswald's psychiatric state, it is possible that if he had lived to face trial, his lawyers would have kept his psychiatric history from being presented in court. He was a

"A Mentally Disturbed Person"

On the day after President Kennedy was assassinated, a New York reporter called psychiatrist Renatus Hartogs to make a statement on television about why someone might kill the president. Unbeknownst to the reporter, Hartogs was the doctor who had given thirteen-year-old Lee Harvey Oswald his psychiatric evaluation when he was placed in the Youth House for truancy in 1953. Hartogs did not mention this coincidence. He later told the Warren Commission what he had said to the reporter concerning the mental health of any individual who would kill a president:

> That a person who would commit such an act has been very likely a mentally disturbed person, who has a personal grudge against persons in authority, and very likely is a person who in his search to overcome his own insignificance and helplessness will try to commit an act which will make others frightened, which will shatter the world, which will make other people insecure, as if he wanted to discharge his own insecurity through his own act, something like that in general terms.

Quoted in "Testimony of Dr. Renatus Hartogs," April 16, 1964, http://mcadams.posc. mu.edu/russ/testimony/hartogs.htm.

teenager at the time and doctor-patient confidentiality rules prevent psychiatrists from testifying against their clients in most cases.

A Young Marxist

Hartogs recommended that Oswald receive extensive psychiatric treatment but before this could happen Marguerite took him back to New Orleans. His grades were still poor when he returned to school and he dropped out after ninth grade.

Despite his lack of formal education, Oswald was a voracious reader who checked out scholarly material from the local library. When he was fifteen, Oswald read *Das Kapital* and *The Communist Manifesto*, two books written by German intellectual Karl Marx in the mid-nineteenth century. Marx wrote about average workers, called the proletariat, and their struggles with factory and farm owners, called the ruling class, or bourgeoisie. Marx believed that the proletariat should take control of all factories and farms and eliminate the ruling class. Everyone in society would then be equal, and all workers would share equally in profits made through the means of production. Followers of Marx, called Marxists, strongly opposed the American capitalist system.

By the time Oswald found Marx's books in the library in 1952, Marxism was widely despised in the United States. The system was associated with the communist government of the Soviet Union, which was considered a major threat to the national security of the United States at that time. Suspected Marxists were fired from their jobs, harassed by the FBI, and were even jailed for their political beliefs. Despite this, Oswald, professed allegiance to Marxism and the Soviet Union. He even wrote a letter to a Marxist youth organization in New York City called the Young People's Socialist League and asked to join.

Oswaldkovich

Despite his interest in Marxism, Oswald was eager to join the military. As Pic put it, "to get from out and under . . . the yolk of oppression from my mother."[58] Although he was only sixteen,

While in the Marines Oswald earned the nickname "Oswaldkovich" because of his interest in the Soviet Union. His Russian stamp book, pictured, was used as evidence of his communist beliefs after the assassination.

Oswald convinced his mother to lie about his age to a Marine recruiter. He was rejected, but still determined to become a Marine. In the following months, Oswald memorized the entire *Marine Corps Manual* and was finally allowed to sign up on his seventeenth birthday.

During his three-year tour of duty in the Marines, Oswald learned to operate radar equipment. He graduated in the top ten of his radar class and was stationed at a military intelligence installation at Atsugi, Japan. This was also the base of one of the largest CIA stations in Asia, home to the agency's chemical, biological, and physiological warfare experiments. Oswald's job at Atsugi was to monitor the flights of top-secret U2 spy planes that were photographing Soviet military installations from high in the sky.

Oswald also took to drinking alcohol while in the Marines and became aggressive and outgoing when drunk. After a minor drunken scuffle in a bar with a fellow Marine, Oswald faced court-martial and was sentenced to thirty days in the brig (jail), where he was made to stand at rigid attention whenever not eating or sleeping. After his release, he was bitter, cold, and withdrawn, telling a fellow Marine, "I've seen enough of a democratic society. When I get out I'm going to try something else."[59]

Some have speculated that his treatment by the Marines caused Oswald to contact Japanese communist agents and offer to become a spy. They point out that Oswald was soon seen taking photographs of buildings and radar equipment around the Atsugi base. In addition, commanders of Oswald's outfit noticed that their top-secret codes had been compromised by Chinese communists.

Oswald was extremely interested in the Soviet Union, and he decided to take a Marine course in Russian. He also subscribed to a Soviet newspaper as well as the American Socialist paper *People's World.* When his shocked commanding officer questioned him about his choice of literature, Oswald said he was trying to understand the enemy. But other members of his unit kidded him about being a spy and called him by a Russian nickname—"Oswaldkovich."

Moving to Moscow

When Oswald was asked by a fellow Marine why he did not go out at night like the other men, he said he was saving his money for something important. And on October 16, 1959, two weeks after receiving an honorable discharge from the Marines, Oswald used that money to defect to the Soviet Union. Whether not he was aided in this task by communist spies remains unknown.

The Warren report attempts to explain Oswald's motives, saying he was unhappy with the United States and chose to move to the Soviet Union in search of a better life. Conspiracy researchers point out, however, that Oswald had been trained to speak Russian during his hitch in the Marines, and since intelligence agents were ostensibly the only people given lessons in Russian, Oswald had been trained as a spy. The State Department did run a program at that time that placed phony defectors within the Soviet Union in order to conduct spying activities. However, in an interview on the TV program *Frontline*, Robert Oswald says he discussed the move with his brother who said he wanted to do something bold and dramatic in the style of bestselling author Ernest Hemingway. Robert Oswald said "He wants to get some experience and write about it."[60] Hemingway had lived in Cuba, Oswald wanted to live in Russia.

The Russians, however, did not seem to trust Oswald in the least. Five days after his defection, a Russian government official refused Oswald's application for citizenship and informed him that he must leave the country immediately. Oswald recorded his feelings and reaction to the news in his diary. He writes:

> I am shocked. . . . I have waited two years to be accepted. My fondest dreams are shattered. . . . I decide to end it. Soak my wrists in cold water to numb the pain, then slash my left wrist. Then plunge wrist into the bathtub of hot water. Somewhere a violin plays as I watch my life whirl away.[61]

Despite Oswald's dramatic description, the cut was not deep and he was in no danger of dying. In the aftermath of the suicide attempt, he was taken to a hospital and given five stitches. The next morning Oswald was transferred to what he called the insanity ward of the hospital, where he was put under close observation for a week by Soviet psychiatrists. Officials determined that he was mentally unstable, but let him remain in the country.

After Oswald was released from the hospital, he traveled to the U.S. Embassy in Moscow and dramatically

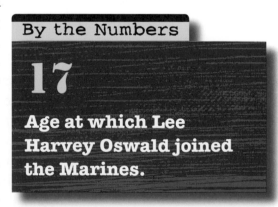

By the Numbers

17

Age at which Lee Harvey Oswald joined the Marines.

renounced his citizenship, turning in his passport to stunned officials. According to former FBI agent and New Orleans district attorney Jim Garrison, "he also announced he would give [the Russians] information about the Marine Corps and the highly secret radar operations he had been involved in [at Atsugi]."[62]

For the next several months, the defector spent his days alone, studying Russian in his hotel room. Then on January 4, 1960, Oswald was given residential papers, which allowed him to remain in Russia as a guest. He was also told he would be transferred to the city of Minsk where he would go to work in a factory. Oswald, however, did not find happiness in his new surroundings. He quickly realized that the Soviet Union was a tightly regimented society where corrupt officials exercised total control over average citizens. After being forced to attend compulsory Communist Party meetings every other day, Oswald wrote "I am starting to reconsider my desire for staying. The work is drab. . . . No night clubs or bowling alleys. I have had enough."[63]

Meeting Marina

In February 1961, the same young man who had angrily renounced his citizenship at the U.S. Embassy wrote a short businesslike letter to the same embassy. Oswald requested the return of his passport and expressed the desire to return home, believing he still retained the full rights of an American citizen. In addition, Oswald wanted to bring his nineteen-year-old wife, Marina Nikolaevna Prusakova, to the United States. The couple had met at a dance hall in Minsk and Marina was quite impressed with Oswald. She thought he was a Soviet citizen because of the way he acted and because he was so fluent in her native language.

When Marina met Oswald, she was living with her uncle, Colonel Ilya Vasilyevich Prusakov. The colonel was a powerful Soviet official who worked in the Ministry of Internal Affairs, a bureau that is similar to the CIA. The couple married and soon had a baby. June Lee Oswald was born on February 15, 1962.

Oswald met his 19-year-old wife Marina while living in the Soviet Union. The couple, along with their infant daughter, moved back to the United States in 1962.

That Oswald was able to court and marry the niece of one of the most powerful men in Minsk has led some researchers to believe that Oswald was at this point a spy working for the Soviets. Others say he was a CIA agent trying to spy on the Soviets by currying favor with a high-level Soviet official. Whatever his true status, the State Department allowed the couple and their infant to return to the United States in May 1962. The American embassy even lent Oswald the money for a "repatriation loan" to move back to the U.S., which can only be made if the recipient's "loyalty to the United States [has been established] beyond question."[64] At this time, Oswald achieved a small degree of notoriety in the press as a Marine who had defected and then returned to the United States.

Hunter of Fascists

After living for a time in New Orleans, the Oswalds moved to Dallas in August 1962. At first the couple socialized with the small anticommunist Soviet community in Dallas, but Oswald was rejected because he was considered loud and obnoxious.

The Soviet Americans were also appalled when they learned that Oswald beat Marina because, as he told Robert, she was "too much like Maw."[65] In his spare time, Oswald struggled to write about his experiences in the Soviet Union. As Robert stated: "He wanted to get his manuscript published if anybody was interested. He had an interesting experience and he had a Russian wife. People ought to take note of this, that he should be interesting."[66]

Failing to write his memoirs, Oswald began looking for a job but his puzzling and erratic behavior continued. In late March 1963, according to Marina, Oswald asked her to take the famous backyard photographs of him holding his rifle and communist newspapers. Marina was reluctant to take what could

Oswald's wife Marina took this famous backyard picture of her husband holding a rifle and communist papers.

be interpreted as incriminating photos, but relented after Oswald explained that he wanted to send one picture to the newspaper the *Militant* and to save the other for June. When she asked him why their young daughter would want a photo of him holding guns, Oswald said, "To remember Papa by sometime."[67] Although Oswald later denied being the subject in the photographs, Marina testified that she took the pictures and even wrote on the back in Russian "Hunter of Fascists Ha. Ha."[68]

In the weeks after the photos were taken, Oswald became obsessed with a popular right-wing leader, retired major general Edwin A. Walker, who lived in Dallas. Walker, a staunch segregationist and anticommunist demagogue, was a controversial figure who often gave speeches at meetings of ultra-right-wing political organizations such as the John Birch Society. Oswald compared Walker to Nazi dictator Adolf Hitler.

According to testimony given to the Warren Commission by Marina, Oswald kept Walker's home under surveillance, and even took several photos of the back of his house. Oswald spent many hours studying maps of Walker's neighborhood and the photos of Walker's house. According to the Warren report, on April 10, 1963, Oswald left home with his Mannlicher-Carcano rifle and traveled to Walker's house. After he had left, Marina discovered the two backyard photos of Oswald, along with a long note, written in Russian. In it Oswald told Marina that he might not return home, and that he paid the rent and utility bills. He told her she could survive for a month or two on his last paycheck from work, which would be waiting in a post office box. He also gave directions to the jail in case he was "taken prisoner."[69] Meanwhile, Oswald was observing Walker through the window of his house as he prepared his income taxes at a desk in his dining room. Around 11 P.M. Oswald allegedly took a shot at Walker but missed. A wooden window frame deflected the bullet and saved the retired general's life.

Oswald returned home panicky and shaken and told Marina what he had done. Although he was frightened that he would be arrested, news reports later confirmed that the police had no suspects.

Oswald was never connected to the shooting until after his death, and then only on the basis of testimony by Marina. With no witnesses and no conclusive evidence there are those who doubt Oswald was involved in the attempted murder of Walker. They allege that Marina, as a Russian immigrant, might have been pressured by the FBI to incriminate her deceased husband. As the Warren report states, the crime made it appear that Oswald was eager to gain notoriety:

> [Oswald had] a strong concern for his place in history. If the attack [on Walker] had succeeded and Oswald had been caught, the pictures showing him with a rifle and his Communist . . . newspapers would probably have appeared on the front pages of newspapers and magazines all over the country.[70]

Traits of Dangerousness

Like many other events tied to the Kennedy assassination, there are divergent opinions concerning the Walker situation. However, it is known that Oswald did seem obsessed with getting his name in the papers. Two weeks after the Walker

Oswald is pictured distributing pro-Cuba flyers in 1962 in the streets of New Orleans, Louisiana. He was vocal about his interest in communism at a time when it was very unpopular.

"The Warren Commission Was Correct"

Psychologists, conspiracy theorists, researchers, and average citizens have argued over Lee Harvey Oswald's guilt or innocence for decades. However, the person who arguably knew him best, his brother Robert Oswald, has little doubt that Lee shot and killed President Kennedy and Officer J.D. Tippit. He made this point clear in an interview for the TV program Frontline:

There is no question in my mind that Lee was responsible for the three shots fired, two of the shots hitting the president and killing him. There is no question in my mind that he also shot Officer Tippit. . . . You look at the factual data, you look at the rifle, you look at the pistol ownership, you . . . look at the general opportunity—he was present. He wasn't present when they took a head count [at the Texas School Book Depository].

You look at all the data there, and it comes up to one conclusion as far as I'm concerned—the Warren Commission was correct. . . . I would love to be able to say that Lee was not involved in any way whatsoever, or much less to the extent that I believe that he was. . . . But the facts are there. . . . True, no one saw him actually pull the trigger on the president but . . . his presence in the building was there. What he did after he left the building is known: bus ride, taxi ride, boardinghouse, pick up the pistol, leave, shoot the police officer. Five or six eyewitnesses there. You can't set that aside just because he is saying, "I'm a patsy." I'd love to do that, but you cannot.

Quoted in *Frontline*, "Who Was Lee Harvey Oswald?" *Frontline*, 1993, www.pbs.org/wgbh/pages/frontline/shows/oswald/interviews/oswald.html.

shooting, he returned to New Orleans where he set up a local branch of the New York City–based Fair Play for Cuba Committee. Working from an office at 544 Camp, Oswald managed the local chapter in which he was the only member.

Promoting the interests of the communist Cuban government was considered highly suspect at this time and Oswald maintained an extremely high profile. He distributed pro-Castro handbills on the street in front of his office. This often provoked vociferous arguments and even several fistfights. Oswald's activity was photographed several times by the press. The attention also landed him a spot on a local radio show. During the interview, Oswald talked intelligently about his interest in communism, Cuba, and the Soviet Union, something few people did in during this era of the cold war.

Little more than seven months after the interview, Oswald was accused of plotting the assassination of JFK. Since Oswald's death, he has been called everything from a pawn and a patsy to a criminal mastermind. But according to Oswald's brother, Robert, at the time of the assassination, Oswald's marriage was failing, his dreams of fame were fading, and he was stuck in a dead-end job. With his Marine training, Soviet defector history, and mental-health problems, Oswald certainly qualified as a troubled loaner with the means to gain international notoriety. Forensic psychologists Ewing and McCann believe Oswald's mental health during his teenage years point to a troubled individual capable of violence. They say "The psychiatric examination of Oswald during his adolescence stands as a portrait of his mental health during a critical period of development."[71] As psychiatrist Hartogs told the Warren Commission: "I found [Oswald] to have definite traits of dangerousness . . . this child had a potential for explosive, aggressive, assaultive [behavior] which was rather unusual to find in a child."[72] Perhaps if Oswald had received proper psychiatric treatment, President Kennedy would have flown back to the White House on November 22, 1963, and finished his term in good health.

Notes

Chapter 1: The Murder of a President

1. Quoted in Harrison Edward Livingstone, *Killing Kennedy and the Hoax of the Century*. New York: Carroll & Graf, 1995, pp. xiii–xiv.

2. Quoted in House Select Committee on Assassinations, "Findings of the Select Committee on Assassinations in the Assassination of President John F. Kennedy in Dallas, Tex., November 22, 1963," House Select Committee on Assassinations, http://jfkassassination.net/russ/jfkinfo/hscareport.htm.

3. Quoted in House Select Committee on Assassinations, "Findings of the Select Committee on Assassinations in the Assassination of President John F. Kennedy in Dallas, Tex., November 22, 1963."

4. Quoted in Anthony Summers, *Conspiracy*. New York: Paragon House, 1989, p. 3.

5. Summers, *Conspiracy*, p. 3.

6. Quoted in Jim Marrs, *Crossfire: The Plot That Killed Kennedy*. New York: Carroll & Graff, 1989, p. 51.

7. Quoted in Vincent Bugliosi, *Reclaiming History*. New York: Norton, 2007, p. 106.

8. Quoted in Norman Mailer, *Oswald's Tale*. New York: Random House, 1995, p. 683.

9. Quoted in Summers, *Conspiracy*, p. 55.

10. Jim Garrison, *On the Trail of the Assassins*. New York: Warner, 1988, p. 22.

11. Quoted in Summers, *Conspiracy*, p. 107.

12. Quoted in Richard Belzer, *UFOs, JFK, and Elvis*. New York: Ballantine, 1999, p. 29.

13. Warren Commission, *Report of the Warren Commission on the Assassination of President Kennedy*. New York: McGraw-Hill, 1964, pp. 41–42.

14. Quote in Summers, *Conspiracy*, p. 493.

Chapter 2: Medical Forensic Mysteries

15. Charles A. Crenshaw, *Trauma Room One: The JFK Medical Coverup Exposed*. New York: Paraview, 2001, pp. 67–68.

16. Quoted in Bugliosi, *Reclaiming History*, p. 71.

17. Quoted in Crenshaw, *Trauma Room One*, p. 76.

18. Quoted in Bugliosi, *Reclaiming History*, p. 110.

19. Charles G. Wilber, *Medicolegal Investigation of the President John*

F. Kennedy Murder. Springfield, IL: Charles C. Thomas, 1978, pp. 94–95.

20. Quoted in Bob Callahan, *Who Shot JFK?* New York: Fireside, 1993, p. 133.

21. Gerald Posner, *Case Closed*. New York: Random House, 1993, p. 300.

22. Wilber, *Medicolegal Investigation of the President John F. Kennedy Murder*, p. 96.

23. Quoted in House Select Committee on Assassinations, "Testimony of Dr. Cyril H. Wecht, Coroner, Allegheny County, Pa.," House Select Committee on Assassinations, http://mcadams.posc.mu.edu/russ/m_j_russ/hscawech.htm.

24. Wilber, *Medicolegal Investigation of the President John F. Kennedy Murder*, p. 102.

25. Quoted in David S. Lifton, *Best Evidence*. New York: Macmillan, 1980, p. 607.

26. Quoted in House Select Committee on Assassinations, "Report of the Select Committee on Assassinations of the U.S. House of Representatives, Section II.—Performance of Autopsy," Kennedy Assassination Home Page, http://mcadams.posc.mu.edu/autopsy3.txt.

27. Wilber, *Medicolegal Investigation of the President John F. Kennedy Murder*, p. 103.

28. Wilber, *Medicolegal Investigation of the President John F. Kennedy Murder*, pp. 6–7.

29. Quoted in Belzer, *UFOs, JFK, and Elvis*, p. 35.

Chapter 3: The Bullets and the Gun

30. Mark Lane, *Rush to Judgment*. New York: Thunder's Mouth Press, 1992, p. 149.

31. Quoted in Lane, *Rush to Judgment*, p. 123.

32. Lane, *Rush to Judgment*, pp. 126–27.

33. Lane, *Rush to Judgment*, p. 128.

34. Lane, *Rush to Judgment*, p. 69.

35. Quoted in Clint Bradford, "Governor Connally's Wrist Wound and CE-399," JFK Assassination Research Materials, August 1999, www.jfk-info.com/fragment.htm.

36. House Select Committee on Assassinations, "Findings of the Select Committee on Assassinations in the Assassination of President John F. Kennedy in Dallas, Tex., November 22, 1963."

37. Warren Commission, *Report of the Warren Commission on the Assassination of President Kennedy*, p. 104.

Chapter 4: Audio Forensics and Evidence on Film

38. Callahan, *Who Shot JFK?*, p. 120.

39. Quoted in Bugliosi, *Reclaiming History*, p. 377.

40. Quoted in Bugliosi, *Reclaiming History*, p. 377.

41. Quoted in Posner, *Case Closed*, p. 457n.

42. Quoted in John McAdams, "Acoustic Evidence of Conspiracy?" Kennedy Assassination, http://mcadams.posc.mu.edu/acoustic.htm#listen.

43. Committee on Ballistic Acoustics, National Research Council, "Reexamination of Acoustic Evidence in the Kennedy Assassination," *Science*, October 8, 1982.

44. Quoted in Belzer, *UFOs, JFK, and Elvis*, p. 15.

45. Warren Commission, *Report of the Warren Commission on the Assassination of President Kennedy*, p. 102.

46. Warren Commission, *Report of the Warren Commission on the Assassination of President Kennedy*, p. 100.

47. House Select Committee on Assassinations, "Findings of the Select Committee on Assassinations in the Assassination of President John F. Kennedy in Dallas, Tex., November 22, 1963."

48. Gary L. Aguilar, "The Converging Medical Case for Conspiracy in the Death of JFK," in *Murder in Dealey Plaza*, ed., James H. Fetzer. Chicago: Catfeet, 2000, p. 184.

49. Belzer, *UFOs, JFK, and Elvis*, pp. 46–47.

Chapter 5: The Mind of Oswald

50. Charles Patrick Ewing and Joseph T. McCann, *Minds on Trial: Great Cases in Law and Psychology*. New York: Oxford University Press, 2006, p. vii.

51. Warren Commission, *Report of the Warren Commission on the Assassination of President Kennedy*, p. 351.

52. Quoted in Warren Commission, *Hearings Before the President's Commission on the Assassination of President Kennedy*, vol. I. Washington, DC: Government Printing Office, 1965, p. 225.

53. Quoted in Warren Commission, *Hearings Before the President's Commission on the Assassination of President Kennedy*, vol. XI, p. 27.

54. Quoted in Warren Commission, *Hearings Before the President's Commission on the Assassination of President Kennedy*, vol. VIII, p. 103.

55. Quoted in Mailer, *Oswald's Tale*, p. 365.

56. Renatus Hartogs, "May 1, 1953 Report of Renatus Hartogs," Akron Community Online Resource Network, www.acorn.net/jfkplace/03/JA/DR/.dr16.html.

57. Ewing and McCann, *Minds on Trial*, p. 24.

58. Quoted in Mailer, *Oswald's Tale*, p. 378.

59. Quoted in Warren Commission, *Hearings Before the President's Commission on the Assassination of President Kennedy*, vol. VIII, p. 112.

60. Quoted in *Frontline*, "Who Was Lee Harvey Oswald?" *Frontline*, 1993, www.pbs.org/wgbh/pages/frontline/shows/oswald/interviews/oswald.html.

61. Quoted in Edward Jay Epstein, *Legend: The Secret World of Lee Harvey Oswald.* New York: McGraw-Hill, 1978, p. 106.

62. Garrison, *On the Trail of the Assassins*, pp. 58–59.

63. Quoted in Epstein, *Legend*, p. 108.

64. Quoted in Garrison, *On the Trail of the Assassins*, p. 59.

65. Quoted in *Frontline*, "Who Was Lee Harvey Oswald?"

66. Quoted in *Frontline*, "Who Was Lee Harvey Oswald?"

67. Quoted in Posner, *Case Closed*, p. 107.

68. Quoted in Edward Jay Epstein, "Question of the Day," http://edward-jayepstein.com/question_oswald2.htm.

69. Quoted in Posner, *Case Closed*, p. 114.

70. Warren Commission, *Report of the Warren Commission on the Assassination of President Kennedy*, p. 406.

71. Ewing and McCann, *Minds on Trial*, p. 26.

72. Quoted in Ewing and McCann, *Minds on Trial*, p. 26.

Glossary

autopsy: The medical examination of a dead body conducted to determine the cause and circumstances of death.

ballistics: The study of firearms, ammunition, and the characteristics of a firearm that affect the way bullets are fired and how they travel.

conspiracy: A plan or agreement between two or more people to commit a crime.

coroner: A public official responsible for investigating suspicious deaths.

forensics: The use of science to investigate a crime.

medical examiner: A licensed physician who specializes in forensic pathology and performs autopsies.

pathology: The scientific study of the nature, origin, stages, and causes of a disease or injury.

patsy: Someone who is manipulated by conspirators to appear guilty for a crime he or she did not commit.

postmortem: An examination of a dead body to determine the cause of death.

sniper: Someone who shoots at people from a concealed position.

trajectory: The path a bullet (or projectile) travels after it is fired from a weapon.

For More Information

Books

Charles A. Crenshaw, *Trauma Room One: The JFK Medical Coverup Exposed*. New York: Paraview, 2001. One of the Texas doctors who examined President Kennedy immediately after his fatal shooting in Dallas talks about his findings, speculations, and the forensic pathology of the case.

Christina Fisanick, ed., *The Bay of Pigs*. Detroit, MI: Greenhaven, 2003. This book provides interesting explanations of the failed Cuban invasion and explores President Kennedy's role and the effect of communism on the U.S. and foreign policies worldwide.

Deborah Heiligman, *High Hopes: A Photobiography of John F. Kennedy*. Washington, DC: National Geographic, 2003. Using photos and text, this book covers Kennedy's life from his childhood to his assassination, including events from his administration such as the Bay of Pigs, the Cuban Missile Crisis, and the establishment of the Peace Corps.

Shelley Sommer, *John F. Kennedy: His Life and Legacy*. New York: HarperCollins, 2005. Illustrated with photographs from the Kennedy Family Collection and the Kennedy Library, this book gives readers a look at a man whose personality and politics helped shape the twentieth century and continue to influence American life.

Patricia M. Stockland, *The Assassination of John F. Kennedy*. Edina, MN: ABDO, 2008. A book of primary sources concerning the murder of President Kennedy, including maps, historic documents, time lines, essential facts, and Web sites.

Josiah Thompson, *Six Seconds in Dallas: A Micro-Study of the Kennedy Assassination Proving That Three Gunmen Murdered the President*. New York: Bernard Geis Associates, 1967. In this frame-by-frame analysis of Abraham Zapruder's film, the author, a veteran criminal investigator, analyzes the filmed record of the event and arrives at a startling conclusion.

DVD

JFK, directed by Oliver Stone. Burbank, CA: Warner Home Video, 2000. The controversial 1991 movie that examines the events leading to the assassination of President John F. Kennedy and alleged subsequent cover-up as seen through the eyes of former New Orleans district attorney Jim Garrison.

Internet Sources

Frontine, "Who Was Lee Harvey Oswald?" *Frontine*, 1993, www.pbs.org/wgbh/pages/frontline/shows/oswald/view. The full three-hour *Frontline* program shown on the fortieth anniversary of Kennedy's murder that explores the enduring mysteries surrounding the president's alleged assassin.

KDFW Fox 4, "JFK Video: The Dallas Tapes," KDFW Fox 4, http://media. myfoxdfw.com/JFKvideo, 2008. Historical footage from Dallas TV station KDFW taken in the aftermath of the Kennedy assassination. Includes footage from Kennedy's arrival in Dallas, Oswald's arrest and subsequent murder, Ruby's trial, interviews with Marina Oswald, and various conspiracies.

National Archives and Records Administration, "The President John F. Kennedy Assassination Records Collection," National Archives and Records Administration, www. archives.gov/research/jfk/index.html. The online collection of more than 260,000 assassination-related records, photographs, and other artifacts mandated for public release by the President John F. Kennedy Assassination Records Collection Act of 1992.

Ralph Thomas, "Example of Digital Evidence and Presentation Backyard Photos Evidence or Fakery," PIMALL, www.pimall.com/nais/news/backyard. html, 2008. Extensive analysis of the photos allegedly showing Lee Harvey Oswald in his backyard with several weapons and communist newspapers. The author contends the pictures were doctored to cast guilt on Oswald.

Web Sites

The John F. Kennedy Assassination Homepage (www.jfk-assassination. de). This site offers articles, photos, and links concerning the Kennedy assassination, including a complete version of the nearly nine-hundred-page Report of the *Warren Commission on the Assassination of President Kennedy*.

Kennedy Assassination Home Page (http://mcadams.posc.mu.edu). A comprehensive Web site with hundreds of pages dealing with nearly every aspect of the Kennedy murder. Dozens of conspiracy theories are explored but the site generally supports the conclusions of the Warren Commission.

Index

Picture Credits

About the Author

Stuart A. Kallen is the prolific author of more than 250 nonfiction books for children and young adults. He has written on topics ranging from the theory of relativity to the history of world music. In addition, Kallen has written award-winning children's videos and television scripts. In his spare time, he is a singer, songwriter, and guitarist in San Diego, California.